IMMUTABLE

Changeless Truth for a Changing World

Randy Lane Bunch

Immutable: Changeless Truth for a Changing World
© 2017 by Randy Lane Bunch

Published by Timothy Publishing Services
3409 W Gary St
Broken Arrow, OK 74012
918-924-6246

Print book ISBN: 978-1-940931-16-6
Ebook ISBN: 978-1-940931-17-3

Library of Congress catalog card number: 2016916932

Printed in the United States of America

"Now, perhaps more than ever, the Church must rise to the challenge of communicating the gospel to a nation adrift, without moorings or moral compass. This cannot be done through argument alone, but through a demonstration of the life and love of God lived out through the Church as a witness to the world."

Randy Lane Bunch

DEDICATION

To my wife, Maria, who continues to spend many hours sleeping on the office floor to be with me while I write. I love you, Baby.

In recent years, God has given me the opportunity to sit under men and women who have helped to open an entirely new world of God's truth to me. I am speaking of Christian apologists, whose job it is to defend the Christian faith, often in hostile, heavily secularized environments that are both difficult and demanding. I am grateful for their efforts and for the fact that God has seen fit to bring me into the sphere of their worthy labors. While not all the essays in this devotional book represent the field of apologetics, their work has served to inform my writing, giving me the understanding and language necessary to reach a world in desperate need of a credible witness for Christ.

TABLE OF CONTENTS

AUTHOR'S PREFACE

This collection of essays has been a labor of love and struggle. Having been written over a period of some years, with each essay appearing first as either a newspaper article, blog entry, or both, it was hard to come up with a title that would communicate a central theme. In the end, the recurring idea of the importance of recognizing eternal, objective truth seemed to stand out as the over-all focus of this body of work. Some ideas are recurrent, and some stories may even be alluded to more than once as these essays were written at different times but sometimes on similar themes.

I have written a lot in the last few years, and many of my essays did not make it into this book. These are offered in the sincere hope that they may be of benefit to the reader. My influences have been many and varied, and I cannot hope to give them all their proper credit. I humbly acknowledge my debt to those whom I have read and continue to read today.

Lastly, this is meant to be a devotional book. The essays follow no particular order and can be read however the reader pleases. It is my profound desire and earnest prayer and that this volume speaks to your heart and helps you come to better know our unchanging God and His immutable truth.

INTRODUCTION

For most of my life, I have communicated to believers as a church planter, pastor, traveling minister, and most recently, as a professor. It is easy to get stuck in our "Christian ghettos" and fail to realize that the world outside is losing interest and withdrawing from the Church. After a while it should become apparent that if this lack of awareness that exists among many believers today is not corrected, we will soon have no one left in our churches to talk to. More than ever, it is crucial for the Church to be able to articulate the biblical worldview in a persuasive, compelling, and relevant way to a culture swiftly moving away from objective truth to embrace a secular worldview.

To do this job effectively, two things must take place. First, believers must live authentic Christian lives that give credibility to the witness we share with the lost world. It was Mahatma Gandhi who was famously reported as saying, "I like your Christ, but not your Christians," expressing what many have echoed about the hollow, superficial, and disingenuous witness of many believers. We simply cannot afford to be saying one thing and living another. It has never been right, of course, but it is lethal to the Christian witness in the highly skeptical culture of today.

Secondly, the Church must be able to articulate the claims of Christianity and the objective truths of scripture in a compelling, convincing, and winsome way. Whether it be through friendly debate, giving our own personal testimony, or the art of storytelling, we must get better at sharing our faith with others. This requires that we know it well and study how to communicate effectively. This should never been seen as optional for a Church commissioned with making disciples of all nations, and yet most believers still feel uncomfortable with the idea of having to defend their faith to their lost friends.

This devotional book is written to hopefully inspire, challenge, inform, and motivate the believer to grow in their walk with God, and at the same time become skilled in communicating their faith to others. If it serves to do this, in even the smallest measure, the author will feel most gratified.

Randy Lane Bunch,
August, 2016

LANDMARKS

Do not remove the ancient landmark which your fathers have set. (Proverbs 22:28)

When looking up the verse above for this article, I was surprised by how much the Bible had to say about these landmarks. The ancient landmarks were the boundaries that divided one man's land from another, and one tribe's inheritance from that of another tribe.

These ancient boundaries provided a set of perimeters in which people could live their lives, raise their families, grow their crops, and enjoy the Lord's blessings. Everything was fine, and the people enjoyed peace, until someone decided to move the lines.

When these ancient boundaries were tampered with, it constituted a violation and could potentially spark a war between neighbors and countrymen. Not only that, it was an affront to God's law given to promote a healthy society. To remove a landmark was to disregard the boundaries that God Himself had set for the people's peace and prosperity. On the right side of the boundary was blessing, but on the wrong side of the boundary was a curse. "Cursed is the one who moves his neighbor's landmark. And all the people shall say, 'Amen!'" (Deuteronomy 27:17).

It seems today that men are once again endeavoring to move the boundaries God has established for society. Whether our world likes it or not, there is little disputing the fact that civil societies are founded on the values reflected in the Word of God. It serves, in fact, as the moral foundation for our justice system. Right and wrong are not ambiguous concepts that can be rewritten at the whim of men who want to inch the old boundaries just north or south of where God has laid them. Truth does not swing back and forth like a pendulum simply because society decides at some point to endorse as good what God condemns as evil. Truth does not swing to the left or the right. It falls like a plumb line.

We understand setting boundaries when it comes to children. In fact, it has become cliché to talk about the out of control child one sees at the Walmart, or the parent who looks like they just fought World War III with their three-year-old, trying to get them to sit down and quit screaming in the shopping cart. We shake our heads and wonder why those parents don't "lay down the law." We understand with children that giving them whatever they want is not love but rather an unhealthy indulgence that will ultimately send them down a path of destruction.

However, when it comes to cultural mores, our society wants to shake itself free from the standards God has given us in His Word for what is good and what is evil. We applaud the "free thinker" who rejects established values. We laugh with the comedian who uses the Church or the Bible as fodder for his or her sardonic wit. Young people that hold to biblical values taught to them by their parents are challenged by the university professor to shake off the shackles of "outdated" morality and embrace the new, progressive mindset that says men are free to write their own code for life and conduct. Simple men and women, who hold to the same strong family values they learned from the previous generation are mocked, marginalized, and ridiculed routinely and with impunity by many in the media.

God, however, is not without a response to this in His Word. He says, "The princes of Judah are like those who remove a landmark; I will pour out My wrath on them like water. Ephraim is oppressed and broken in judgment, *because he willingly walked by human precept*" (Hosea 5:10-11, *emphasis mine*). In another place He says, "The kings of the earth prepare to fight, and their leaders make plans together against the LORD and his appointed one. They say, 'Let's break the chains that hold us back and throw off the ropes that tie us down.' But the one who sits in heaven laughs; the Lord makes fun of them" (Psalm 2:2-4 *NCV*).

I would imagine that God's reaction to the prevailing hostility exhibited by many toward His standards of right and wrong is similar to the one that makes us shake our heads at those out of control children we often see today. Men may scream and shake their fists at the heavens, but their frustration with God's righteous standard doesn't change what is right or wrong any more than a child pushing against the side of his house makes the world rotate in a different direction.

In the end, we need to realize that God did not put boundaries on men because He wanted to limit their fulfillment in life, but to protect them from the dangers that lay on the wrong side of the line. In fact, He sent His Son to die for us that His laws could be written on our hearts, not binding or restricting us, but bringing us into the glorious liberty that comes with knowing the love of a Father who cares for us enough to lead us away from harm.

FIXER UPPERS

He heals the brokenhearted
And binds up their wounds. (Psalm 147:3)

God is in to "fixer-uppers." He likes to fix things. I have a southern heritage, though I was the only one in my immediately family that was born in California. A Louisiana woman and a Mississippi man raised me. Both of my sisters were also Mississippi born and grew up in their younger years in the state of Louisiana. My Dad used to love to say that I was the only "prune picker" in the bunch! I suppose that was a reference to California's agricultural strength (I really have no idea, but he loved to say it). However, I definitely picked up some of their southern colloquialisms in my speech. One of those was the word *fixin'*. I was never "about to do" this or that. I was always "fixin' to do" this or that. It wasn't until years later that someone in New England, quite amused at the expression, pointed out that it wasn't a common usage of the word, so far as they knew (which shows you just how little those New Englanders know). If you were raised in a southern home, you know exactly what I mean, and probably even know what it means when your mother told you that you were going to have a dinner with "all the fixin's"!

Well, God is in to fixin' too! Like any good parent, He knows kids are going to break things. God had hardly turned His creation over to us when we broke it! We know the story well enough about how our original parents sinned against God, creating a breach in our relationship with Him. However, as catastrophic as this was, God already had a plan in place to fix what man had broken. It would take a masterstroke to fix so broken a world, and in fact, it would take great sacrifice on God's part. Some things are costly to repair. That is why Jesus is called the "Lamb slain from the foundation of the world" (Revelation 13:8). We broke the world in which we live and lost ourselves in the process, but Jesus came to heal the broken, as well as "to seek and save that which was lost" (Luke 19:10). Jesus' death bridged the gap and healed the rift between holy God and sinful man, and now our broken fellowship with God is restored.

In the latter part of 2013, Pastor Billy Rash of Kern Christian Center in Bakersfield asked my wife and I to plant an extension work in our home town of Taft, California. The vision of Kern Christian Center had always included satellite churches, and so in February of 2014, West Kern Christian Center was launched. Someone has well said that young churches are like rockets; the largest part of the fuel is used up just getting off the pad! Like most young churches starting in modern America, we struggled in the early days to find our feet.

As I was praying about this one day, asking God to send us helpers, He began to speak to me about what we were called to do in our community. He spoke to me about the broken condition, not merely in the world, but in the lives of many believers. Sometimes the brokenness comes from the poor choices and bad decisions of the individual. Sometimes others break us through mishandling when we're too young and vulnerable to defend ourselves and to naïve to be aware of the damage that is being done. Sometimes people are simply victims of circumstance and end up being raised by those whose love and care is not equal to that of a lost parent. Too real in our day is the horrific damage that is done by drugs, a grim reaper that robs children of happiness and home, sometimes even crippling their start in life as they struggle with the physical damage done to them in the womb by addicted parents. And not all damage is done when we're young. This world can continue to inflict its cruel blows to those who have already had set backs in life as they struggle to deal with broken relationships, financial challenges, or even deep depression.

My prayer time that day had started with me asking for help. God's response concluded with what He wanted me to do to help others. He said He would send in the troops, and then He showed me a wounded, weary, lone soldier coming into view with his helmet slid back, his steps slow and faltering, with his rifle dragging the ground behind him. The Lord said to me, "These are your troops. I'll send them in by the ones and twos. You'll need to tend to their wounds." God has often dealt with the walking wounded, and He loves to heal them, even those whose wounds are self-inflicted.

The fact is, God knows a good investment when He sees one. He's made a career of making much out of broken down lives. Some of His best work has been done in the lives of broken men who knew the bitter taste of personal failure. Moses, David, Peter, and Paul the apostle were all at some point in their lives such men, but God so worked in them that their lives became trophies of grace for all the world to see. This is why God is not bothered by broken people. He knows exactly what to do with them, if they'll allow Him to do the fixin'.

I recently had another conversation with Pastor Billy in his office, and I was surprised to hear what God had said to him when he first planted the church in Bakersfield, nearly 30 years ago. God told him, "Many of my people are broken, and you will have to repair, restore, revive, and ultimately, release them." God does not want us to live broken lives, but neither is He ashamed of our brokenness. He'll take our shattered lives and make a masterpiece of grace that will give the promise of happiness, healing, and hope to a broken world.

FEAR NOT

For God has not given us a spirit of fear and timidity, but of power, love, and self- discipline. (2 Timothy 1:7 *NLT*)

Some of the younger generation may not be too familiar with the phrase "Y2K", but many of us still remember that trendy acronym (which stood for Year 2000) and the global panic surrounding it. There was great fear from many sectors of the business and financial world that when we entered the new millennium our computers would not be able to handle the change of the clock. Everything from a global financial meltdown to international businesses collapsing to mass starvation in the streets was prophesied by the talking heads of the day. In the end, nothing came of it.

People that had spent money on canned food, bottled water, and emergency rations were living on tuna fish and pork and beans for the next several months, wondering why the sky had not fallen. When the proverbial dust settled from the huge non-event, none of the news outlets that had helped promote the pandemonium issued apologies or acknowledged they had gotten it wrong. Apocalyptic prophets, both secular and spiritual, crawled back into their bunkers, still shaking their heads and warning that the big day of doom was yet to come.

In reality, fear sells. There's nothing like a potential crisis to stir the ratings of television news shows and boost newspaper sales. Politicians get elected playing on the fears of people, and pharmaceutical companies sell drugs to keep you from getting horrible sounding diseases you've never heard of. The global economy rises or falls on fears of what may or may not happen, and everyone is afraid of what tomorrow holds.

The Bible says that Satan is the "god" of this world (2 Corinthians 4:4). In this context, the "world" is not the planet we live on so much as it represents the system or sphere in which fallen men live their lives. Satan, who has used fear as his stock and trade since we first see him make his entrance in the scriptures, rules over the hearts of men still alienated from God because of sin. When one understands this, it begins to make perfect sense why the decisions of so many people in this world are motivated by fear. In fact, we are constantly being told of more things we should be afraid of every day: global warming, gun violence, North Korea, and on and on the list goes.

It's interesting that the Bible never caters to a fear-based philosophy for life. You never see Jesus nervous or cryptically telling the disciples to buy "tribulation rations" and find a good cave in which to hide. On the contrary, after giving a list of frightening things that will come on the earth in the last days, Jesus said, "Now when these things begin to happen, look up and lift up your heads, because your redemption draws near" (Luke 21:28). In another place He says, "And you will hear of wars and rumors of wars. See that you are not troubled..." (Matthew 24:6). Whenever angelic visitors would bring messages to the frightened men and women who beheld them, their message seemed to invariably begin with, "Fear not," and David famously said, "Yea, though I walk through the valley of the shadow of death, I will fear no evil; For You are with me; Your rod and Your staff, they comfort me" (Psalm 23:4).

The apostle John said, "There is no fear in love; but perfect love casts out fear" (1 John 4:18). That perfect love was expressed when Jesus bore our sins on Calvary's cruel cross and died so that we might be reconciled to God. Now, though we are *in* this world, the Bible says that we who are in Christ are "not of this world" (John 17:14-15), and we are not to be ruled by fear but by the Word of God. God is faithful and His Word is true, and in the end, this is not our final destination. We are just sojourners here, and our eyes are not fixed on this world which is passing away but on that eternal habitation where nothing can hurt or destroy.

RESTORING OUR CULTURAL CONSCIENCE

Righteousness exalts a nation,

But sin is a reproach to any people. (Proverbs 14:34)

I believe America is dangerously close to the total and complete bankruptcy of her moral conscience. To continue heading in the same direction, caving to the purveyors of political correctness (who define "correctness" as appeasing the demands of the most recently offended special interest group), not to mention the moral relativism that pervades our society, would be to slip off the precipice and into a moral abyss from which it is difficult to imagine a recovery. To anyone with a biblical worldview, it would seem that we are inexorably heading into dark and dangerous waters, despite the fact that many seem to recognize the problem and are desperately trying to turn the ship around. It's like one of those dreams in which you're trying to shout out a warning but have no voice. There seems to be a groupthink among our intellectual elite and cultural influencers that holds to the idea that to espouse moral absolutes, to suggest that people be held accountable for their choices, is itself a crime and the very height of social indecency.

I am not sure how we got here. We are a mere quarter century removed from the fall of Communism, which left both Russia and the Soviet Bloc nations spiritually, culturally and financially destitute, and we have those in our nation who are getting political traction campaigning from an unapologetic platform of socialism. It's utterly unbelievable. Even worse, just fifteen years after 9/11, we have those in power who seem to feel that the answer is to terrorism is to ignore the threat of radical Islam, kowtowing to tyrants rather than taking positive and decisive action against those who have tortured and slaughtered the innocent and want to destroy our way of life as well. The innocent suffer while the wicked thrive due to our complacency and half measures to stop them. How many beheadings do we have to see on our social media sites, or mass shootings in our streets, before we say, "Enough is enough," and put a stop to this madness?

What happened to us? Where are our moral convictions? Where is our heart? Where are the real statesmen, like Churchill and Reagan, who have a clear understanding of the times, a positive vision for their nation, and who are not confused about who the good guys and the bad guys are? And yes, there really are bad guys out there; people who want to promote their ideology at the expense of everyone else's life and liberty. When Churchill faced such aggressors, embodied in his day by the Nazi's, there was no confusion as to the course Britain had to take. It was win or be destroyed. When Reagan declared there to be an "Evil Empire," referring to the USSR, there was no ambiguity about who and what he meant. He met the challenge to freedom head on and ultimately triumphed. Such leaders inspire those they lead, rallying and unifying their nations behind them.

When we fail to stand for something, we fall for anything. We become the victims of the newest bully on the block, which at this time is ISIS and other radical Islamic groups, who seem dead set on subjugating the West and bringing us under the control of a global Islamic caliphate. Europe is being hit like a tsunami now, and there are leaders there who are afraid that the battle is already lost. Likewise, our own national resolve is weak, and that, to those who are not confused about their objective, is like the smell of blood in the water. It is our lack of clear conviction and moral character which robs us of the courage and resolve necessary to act. But I do not believe it is too late.

If ever there was a time when a nation was completely, morally destitute, it was late 18th Century Britain. Child prostitution, violence, slavery, and corruption were the order of the day. Even forms of animal cruelty far worse than our modern day dog fighting, were considered an acceptable form of entertainment for the poor, uneducated masses. However, as dark as things were, God had an answer to this moral crisis.

Into this time and place, He raised up men like John and Charles Wesley, George Whitfield, and John Newton: preachers who helped to restore the crumbling biblical foundation of Great Britain, calling their nation back to Christ. Alongside these men was the unquenchable MP, William Wilberforce, and his friends known as the Clapham Sect, a group of wealthy and highly influential Christian friends with whom he collaborated and who, by their tireless efforts, helped him to achieve his two great objectives: to bring about the "reformation of manners" (what we would today call morals), and the suppression of the slave trade in Great Britain. To these ends they were successful, not only seeing sweeping social reforms pass into law that completely changed the complexion of their nation, but ultimately seeing the abolition of slavery in Great Britain, way ahead of our own nation which would not achieve this without the bloodiest of civil wars.

Wilberforce alone, who was largely forgotten and unknown in our nation until the recent movie, *Amazing Grace*, resurrected his memory and brought awareness to his great accomplishments, was a veritable force of nature. Standing only five feet tall, he became without question the most gigantic figure of his time on the political scene. A sickly and frail child, Wilberforce would suffer from the debilitating effects of Colitis all his life, only finding relief from the opiate, laudanum. The drug, however, never dulled his evangelical zeal once his lost faith was recovered in his early manhood. Thinking a career in politics to be out of step with a life of godliness, he considered entering the ministry until his friend and mentor, John Newton, author of the hymn, *Amazing Grace*, encouraged him to serve God by continuing to serve his nation as a Member of Parliament. In so doing, Newton did the world an enormous favor, as the reforms that Wilberforce would achieve quite literally changed the course of his nation and the world. His influence, though seldom credited, is unquestionably still felt in western civilization today. However, he would be the first to say that he did none of this on his own. He was surrounded by likeminded individuals whose commitment to their cause was as unflagging as his own.

We need that same spirit in our nation today. There is a cause worth standing for in our times. We need our nation called back to the biblical foundations of liberty that made her great. What made us great then can make us great again, but it takes men and women equal to the task who are willing to speak up and let their voice be heard, both before the throne of grace and in the public square. If not now, never. This is America's last, best chance to recover something of the greatness that made her the model of democracy the world over. This is not about being a proud American, but about being a humble believer who knows that our hope is not in ourselves, but in the God who once shed His grace upon our nation.

ACCESS

For we do not have a High Priest who cannot sympathize with our weaknesses, but was in all points tempted as we are, yet without sin. Let us therefore come boldly to the throne of grace, that we may obtain mercy and find grace to help in time of need. (Hebrews 4:15-16)

As I am sitting here writing this piece, I am suffering the frustrations of a broken internet connection. On the other side of the world in Pakistan, a group of young, new believers are waiting to hear a word of encouragement and for me to pray for them via Skype. Their dear pastor and I are communicating back and forth, using my iPad's cellular connection, waiting for online communications to be restored.

As I thought of this, my mind went immediately to the connection we have with our heavenly Father, a connection that is never down or broken. That connection is not available through fiber optic cables or a cellular plan, but only through the blood of Christ, shed on our behalf to repair the "broken line" between heaven and earth.

God spoke to men in the Old Testament before Christ died to redeem us, but it was an imperfect connection in that even those who were considered to be His people did not have their own direct line to God. They had to wait until God spoke through the prophet to hear what the Lord wanted to say to them. Likewise, they could not communicate directly to God, but had to go through the priests and a series of sacrifices designed to maintain the level of connection available to them at that time.

Under the Old Covenant, even God's priests were separated from the Ark of the Covenant and the Mercy Seat by a veil that hung as a continual reminder that man did not yet have access to the presence of God. Only on the Day of Atonement did the High Priest enter the Holy of Holies to present the blood of the Passover Lamb on the Mercy Seat, to make atonement for the sins of the people. As I look at my Internet connection, which is still down, there is exclamation mark over the Wi-Fi icon with the words "limited connection" next to it. That is a good image to symbolize the kind of connection that sinful man had with a holy God in the Old Covenant. God had to hold man at a distance lest he be consumed in His presence.

It is not so now. God gave us a tremendous connection upgrade when Christ died on Calvary to secure our eternal redemption. In fact, at the moment of His death, that veil in the temple was torn in two, from the top to the bottom, to signify that God had restored man's lost connection with Himself (see Matthew 27:50-51). Now each and every one of us have our own direct line to the throne of grace that we might worship God, know intimacy with Him, and have access to His mercy and grace in our times of need.

The price for this connection was not a two-year contract with a local service provider. This was no short-term arrangement God made for us. Jesus became a man to identify with us, bear our sin, and to serve as our High Priest forever! It was His very flesh that was torn, just like that veil in the temple, that opened a line of connection with God that those in the Old Testament could only dream of.

> Therefore, brethren, having boldness to enter the Holiest by the blood of Jesus, by a new and living way which He consecrated for us, through the veil, that is, His flesh, and having a High Priest over the house of God, let us draw near with a true heart in full assurance of faith, having our hearts sprinkled from an evil conscience and our bodies washed with pure water. (Hebrews 10:19-22)

We need no further sacrifice to approach the throne of God. The sacrifice of Jesus satisfied our debt, balanced the scales of divine justice, and restored our connection with God. Now He is available to us around the clock. There are no surprise charges or extra hoops to jump through to have uninterrupted service. There is no need to face the dark hour alone or feel that God is holding you at a distance. He is truly just a call away. In fact, if you have lost your connection with God personally, Paul assures us that "…whoever calls on the name of the Lord shall be saved" (Romans 10:13). Call on Him now. Jesus is your access to the Father, and you'll never get a busy signal or get disconnected.

LIMITS

For I say, through the grace given to me, to everyone who is among you, not to think of himself more highly than he ought to think, but to think soberly, as God has dealt to each one a measure of faith. (Romans 12:3)

It is wise for all of us to know our limitations. We all have limits to our talents, abilities, understanding and knowledge. God, too, has set limits on us. He has not gifted or "graced" us to do it all. The context of Paul's admonition, as you read on, is in reference to our personal gifts and offices of service in the Church. In the verses that follow, he says, "Having then gifts differing according to the grace that is given to us, let us use them..." (Romans 12:6). The fact that the grace differs for each of us is evidence that none of have it all. We all have limits.

There are some things I know I can do. That is not a boast. It is confidence in His grace on my life. There's a measure of faith I have to step out and serve God with the abilities He has given me. I know that when I step into the pulpit, His ability will enable me to deliver His Word with power. It is that confidence, that "measure of faith," that Paul refers to that gives expression to the grace of God He has entrusted to me. Paul says we are not to think more highly of ourselves than we ought, but to realize that we are limited to a *measure* of faith.

Every believer has some grace or giftedness from God (see Ephesians 4:7). We are to steward that by using it to build up and edify the Church (see Ephesians 4:16). God has made an investment in each of our lives, and He is looking for a return on His investment. As Peter says so succinctly, "As each one has received a gift, minister it to one another, as good stewards of the manifold grace of God" (1 Peter 4:10).

So far so good. The rub comes when we begin to look at our *lack* of ability in certain areas and become disheartened, or even envious, because we cannot do what others can. Sadly, there are those who live their whole lives frustrated in God's service because they wrongly assume that because they cannot serve God in the same fashion that someone else does, God has somehow shortchanged them.

I want to drop a thought in your mind that maybe you've never considered before. *Forget about your limitations!* No, I'm not talking about moral weaknesses or areas of our lives we need to submit to the sanctifying work of the Holy Spirit, but rather those areas where we don't seem to be particularly gifted. There's a good reason why you can't do certain things. You're limited. So am I.

This is counter-intuitive to our thinking in the West because we've all heard that good parents tell their children, "You can do anything you set your mind to." The fact is, we *can't* do whatever we set our minds to, and to think that we can *will* ourselves into abilities, natural or God-given, that we do not possess is to set ourselves up for frustration and disappointment.

Too often in the church we spend time trying to be a better singer, a better speaker, a better leader, or whatever it is that others do, while looking past that which *we* do really well and for which we are obviously gifted. We've heard a lot about thinking *outside* the box, and there's a time to do that in regard to creative problem solving, but when it comes to these matters, we need to be looking *inside* the box at what we already have, appreciating the gifts and abilities God has entrusted to us.

When we stand before the judgment seat of Christ, we will not give an account for what we *weren't* called or gifted to do. God will ask, "What have you done with what you've been given?" We will have either been faithful, investing His gift into the purpose for which He gave it, or we'll be like the wicked and slothful servant in Matthew's parable that hid his Master's talent in the ground (see Matthew 25:14-30).

The longer I serve God, the more comfortable I am with all the things I *can't* do. God has entrusted me with what He saw fit to give me that I might serve Him acceptably. If I'm diligent with that, I can stand before Him with boldness, knowing that I have been a good and faithful steward.

Embracing our limitations helps to us appreciate the gifts in others. It also helps us to narrow our focus and be more effective in developing ourselves where God has truly called us. So, instead of trying to improve our weaknesses, I believe we need to soar with our strengths, learning to steward well the grace God has given us. Doing so will help us grow in confidence as we serve God in the sweet spot of His ability in our lives.

MOMENTS

For our light affliction, which is but for a moment, is working for us a far more exceeding and eternal weight of glory,
while we do not look at the things which are seen, but at the
things which are not seen. For the things which are seen are
temporary, but the things which are not seen are eternal.
(2 Corinthians 4:17-18)

We put much into this life. We invest years into cultivating
our careers, educating our minds, and making our mark.
We are a busier people today than ever before despite all the conveniences we have that are designed to save us time. In reality, they
only minimize our labor in one area so we can increase our activity in
another. We are, to say the least, a people on the go, and the moments
pass by. Moments that are intended to serve as opportunities to
invest into things of eternal significance are squandered on temporal
achievements that will likely be forgotten by the next generation, or
in a decade, a year, or even a moment.

The scripture says that Satan has blinded the minds of those who
do not believe the gospel (2 Corinthians 4:4). It turns out that he is

not only a master at deception, but of distraction as well. He keeps our minds off of eternal matters, matters of true consequence, by offering worldly pleasures that titillate the senses but do not satisfy the soul. For many, the discovery comes too late that having all the success, pleasure, and fame this world offers leaves one no more satisfied than the one who is still preoccupied by his pursuit of them. It is all a phantom with no substance, like a beautifully wrapped package that is empty of any treasure.

We live for the moment, putting all our focus on instant gratification with little thought for the long-range consequences of squandering away our lives, until, in the end, there are no moments left. We immerse ourselves in the subtle, superficial seductions of the *now* while anesthetizing ourselves to our own mortality. One day it will come to an end, and all our moments will have been spent. The real question is, "What will our spent moments have purchased for us?" What will be the final tally at the end? What reward will we have for the lives we have lived?

"Life is short" is not merely a cliché. The longer one lives the truer that reality becomes. Life becomes more urgent the older we become, and we realize we have less road before us than we do behind us. A wise person takes stock of his life and begins to evaluate his priorities. The truth is, however, that age does not always equal wisdom, and not all people who grow older become more thoughtful. It is easy to delude oneself into thinking that there's always more moments to come. As a pastor, I have known a number of people who came to faith late in life after realizing that they were missing something in their lives. I am glad they came to know the Lord and gave their latter years in service to Him, but I have no doubt that if they could they would say (and I have indeed heard some say) that they only wished they had begun their spiritual journey sooner.

This can be as true for believers as for unbelievers. It is always easy to assume that we will have time to get around to spiritual priorities later. Once, when I was reading in the book of James in the New Testament, I came across the passage which says, "For what is your life? It is even a vapor that appears for a little time and then vanishes away" (James 4:14). The Lord said to me through that verse, "One of the reasons my people waste so much time is because they live as though they had an unlimited supply of it." The fact is, we all have an expiration date on our lives. What is even ninety or one hundred years in the light of eternity? We have only a moment to plan for forever.

The Bible says of believers, "For we must all appear before the judgment seat of Christ, that each one may receive the things done in the body, according to what he has done, whether good or bad" (2 Corinthians 5:10). No, our works do not get us into Heaven. Eternal life is a gift of God's grace we receive through faith in Christ's redeeming work, but we *will* give an account before Christ for how we used the moments with which we were entrusted. In the end, all of us, believer and unbeliever alike, will have to reckon with how we managed our moments.

The apostle Paul chose to live his life to the fullest for Christ. He had many dangerous and difficult moments, as he paid a great price to fulfill the call of God upon his life. He suffered persecution from both the Gentiles as well as his own countrymen. Ultimately, he met his end on the Apian Way somewhere outside of Rome, a martyr for the Lord he loved and the message he lived to share. However, none of this moved Paul. He knew that no matter how great the suffering, it was only for a moment. The reward, on the other hand, was eternal.

I asked God to help me make my fifties my most fruitful decade yet. I believe that is a prayer He can honor. He has given me many opportunities already to invest into the lives of others. It is a rewarding life. Jesus must have known what He was talking about when He said, "It is more blessed to give than to receive" (Acts 20:35). My moments are very precious to me. In one sense, they are no more precious now than they've ever been, except in the fact that there are fewer of them left to me now than when I started this race. Nevertheless, whether you're young, middle-aged, or older, learn to make the most of your moments by investing them into something bigger than yourself. God has a part for you to play in His plan, and if you will give yourself to His purpose for your life, I promise you won't regret it—not even for a moment.

A PLACE CALLED HOME

God gives the lonely a home. (Psalm 68:6 *New Century Version*)

Years ago, the theme song to the popular TV show, *Cheers,* quipped that we all want to go "where everybody knows your name." I think that is one of the most fundamental and universal needs of the human heart. To have a place we call "home," where we are always recognized, always welcomed, and always loved. For those of us who have known such a place at one time in our lives, we will always be trying to rediscover it (if we've lost it), or at the least, recreate it at another place and time with another group of people.

The famous writer, Thomas Wolfe, once said, "You can't go home again." Most of us with a little life experience behind us have probably felt that sense of displacement Wolfe was referring to. We may go back home after a year away at school, a term of military service, or after years of living elsewhere to see that our Norman Rockwell-like picture of home was not freeze-framed while we were away. Life went on for those we left behind. Some of the faces aren't in the picture anymore, and others have come in their place. The friends we used to spend the afternoons with are now gone, married, or otherwise occupied with life's pursuits. It's still home, and yet it isn't – not like we remember it.

Sometimes that displacement is even greater when divorce breaks a family apart and the pieces of the once tranquil family life go flying in all directions, never to be reassembled in the same way again. Forgiveness and healing may come, but the family dynamic is irreparably changed. On many, the shrapnel from the explosion leaves a permanent mark that never fully goes away. Scars of distrust and uncertainty about life remain. Home ceases to mean the same thing, as it becomes redefined by new people entering the family dynamic.

For some, the idea of home has never been associated with warmth and love but rather with danger, pain, and fear. Alcoholism, addiction, and abuse robbed them of the love and security that home was supposed to provide. Escape became the only option for those too young to understand what was wrong with mommy or daddy, or to defend themselves from the violence of which they became the target. Today, more and more "mommies and daddies" are really grandmothers and grandfathers, raising their grandchildren and trying to pick up the pieces after their addicted or imprisoned children.

Regardless of the image that "home" conjures up in our minds, we all know inherently what it is *supposed* to look like. One of the most powerful images of this I have ever seen in cinema was portrayed in the Denzel Washington directed movie, *Antwone Fisher*, a true story about a young black man's dream to find a real home, free of the violence and abuse he suffered in his foster home. The movie starts with the image of a large family table, spread with every homemade dish one could wish for, with a welcoming family standing behind it, ready to shower young Antwone with love and praise.

The image, as it turns out, is a dream, and it would be years before Antwone would find in reality what he had dreamt of his whole life.

I found an interesting quote of Antwone Fisher's on the internet which is as follows: "Brenda Profitt was my elementary school teacher. She was the first adult I ever trusted. She spoke to all of us the same way. It was a tone of respect. And I wasn't accustomed to being spoken to that way. I think that being with her for three years made all the difference. So whatever it was that she possessed, that she gave to us, we kept."[1]

To my mind, what Brenda Profitt gave to Antwone was a true sense of what *home* is to be like. Antwone finally found his home and family (at least in the movie version of his story), but for millions of disenfranchised people the notion of home is still an enigma, and the reality of it, undiscovered.

Enter Jesus. He dealt with the lonely and disenfranchised throughout his life and ministry, giving them love and understanding, as well as that all-important sense of personal value that comes with acceptance and an awareness of purpose for one's life. Jesus never reduced people. He always enlarged them, showing them their potential in the light of God's love, releasing them from the prison of their dark and loveless lives to a new day full of hope. In turn, they became emissaries of that same divine love that they had themselves received.

For my part, it is my desire to do for others through the love and grace of God and the power of the Holy Spirit, what Brenda Profitt did for Antwone Fisher. More than that, I want to do for others what Jesus did for those He encountered. As a pastor, I want the church I lead to be that place "where everybody knows your name" and is glad to see you whenever you arrive; not just the clean and tidy, but all those whose lives have been ravaged by the harshness of this world. In short, we want to be the kind of church in which the lonely can find a home.

SEASONS

Brothers and sisters, I myself don't think I've reached it, but I do this one thing: I forget about the things behind me and reach out for the things ahead of me. (Philippians 3:13 *Common English Bible New Testament*)

O ften as we start our journey, we never think about how transitory many aspects of life really are. We assume that the people, places, and things in our lives today are permanent fixtures in the backdrop of our life. Most don't live with a day-to-day awareness, particularly in youth, that many of the things we enjoy in life today have an expiration date and will one day be gone. Friends move, jobs change, and new opportunities take us to different places from where we started.

In fact, the inconstancy of life is one of its most constant features. Change happens all around us, all the time. The sooner we embrace this as normal and necessary to life, the sooner we are able to transition from one season of life to the next with grace and anticipation for the new adventure that awaits. The fear of change is common, almost universal, and usually has something to do with our desire to hang on to what we have, our reluctance to adapt or to learn new things, and a general uncertainty of the future.

However, change is necessary in the process of life. We don't want change merely for change's sake, but we do need to understand that moving forward in the plan of God will often mean saying farewell to one season of our lives and embracing another. While we instinctively want to hold on to those who played a major role in a prior season, the impracticality of maintaining the same closeness often means they move into more of a background role in our lives, as new relationships and involvements relative to the new season we are entering come into the foreground.

Such a life, moving with the purposes of God, becomes a rich tapestry of layered experience and relationships that deepen our wisdom and understanding of life. Our myopic views open to a broader understanding of the larger world, enabling us to become more versatile and relate more widely. In my own experience, I have found that each new season I have entered has benefitted from the collective experience and wisdom of the previous seasons, making my contribution greater as I continue to move forward in my life's journey. Our value to the world around us, and those whom we serve, deepens as our own interior borders are extended through our growth, breaking us loose from our prior confines and maturing us in ways we could never have anticipated. As we look into the reservoir of our experience, there is so much more to draw from and pass on to the generation that must take the baton from us.

Learning to cooperate with the changing seasons, rather than resisting them, is essential to our success and enjoyment of the journey. Life is not static but fluid, and change will come regardless of our reluctance or acceptance, so we must learn to stay adaptable. Sometimes change will come naturally, as a normal consequence of life, while at other times we will have to be more intentional about making changes, as we learn to cooperate with the transition from one season to the next. Sometimes change is initiated by God, as He moves us into position to serve His ongoing purpose for our lives.

The truth is that change keeps something alive and young in us that can otherwise be lulled to sleep by the all too familiar rhythms of a comfortable season that fails to present new challenges. God's not done with you yet, which likely means more new seasons are still ahead of you, along with a still richer life from which you will have even more wisdom and experience to share with others.

DISTRACTIONS

Jesus said, "Come off by yourselves; let's take a break and get a little rest." (Mark 6:31 *The Message Bible*)

M ost of the time, distractions are thought of as a bad thing. We do not want to get distracted from whole-heartedly serving the Lord, pursuing His plan for our lives, or from those worthy pursuits that require focus and intentionality.

However, life is not a sprint. It is the marathon of all marathons, and no one can run "all out" for the entire race. We are still human, and we all share certain natural limitations. We can push ourselves too hard, burn out mentally or physically, and end our run prematurely if we don't learn to appreciate distractions. For you it may be reading a book, taking a walk, or rolling on the carpet with the kids. For others it may be some quiet time in a cabin, far away from the fast paced, frenetic tempo of business. Others might like the water; looking out at the ocean or lounging by a pool or lake.

We need distractions from our pursuits, no matter how noble or important, if we are to run the race before us with endurance. Some of us are fortunate enough to do the things we love for a living. We may not feel the need for distraction in the same way others do because we find our work refreshing and fulfilling. However, chances are there are others in our lives who need us to get distracted for a while. If we don't stop to appreciate the gift of our loved ones, we may leave them behind in the cold shadow of our ambitions.

The truth is, none of us are the Savior. Some of us can get pretty intense and take ourselves a little too seriously, forgetting that the world rotated on its axis every single day before we came on the scene to save it, and will likely continue doing so long after we are gone. That's not to say our endeavors are not important, but regardless of what they are, we need to realize that they do not make the world go 'round. Millions upon millions of people will live and die and never know our names or appreciate our accomplishments. All the more reason to cherish those who appreciate us, not for what we do, but for who we are, and realize that God, too, is more interested in us than He is our service.

I take what I do very seriously, but I sometimes have to be reminded not to take myself too seriously. When I fail in this, which I occasionally do, I have others around me that will smile, wink at each other, pat me on the head, and tell me it's all going to be okay. It takes me a moment sometimes to let my pace slacken, join in on the joke, and realize they are right. God surrounds us with such people because He loves us too much to let us think we're big enough to do His job. In fact, next time you're seeking Him for the great unfolding of His purpose, He might just tell you to take a walk, chill out, and come back after you've had a chance to get distracted.

It took some of us a long time to learn these lessons. Some of us are still learning, and our prayer for you is that you learn to live a balanced life; full of purpose, yes, but also full of the memories that are only made in the lighter moments of life, surrounded by those you love. So, if you're at your wits end or running a little too hard and fast, take some time to get distracted for a while. You may even find that a few moments of well-earned distraction today, make you better prepared to tackle the problems of tomorrow.

THE GOD WHO ANSWERS BY FIRE

And it came to pass, at the time of the offering of the evening sacrifice, that Elijah the prophet came near and said, "Lord God of Abraham, Isaac, and Israel, let it be known this day that You are God in Israel and I am Your servant, and that I have done all these things at Your word. Hear me, O Lord, hear me, that this people may know that You are the Lord God, and that You have turned their hearts back to You again." Then the fire of the Lord fell and consumed the burnt sacrifice, and the wood and the stones and the dust, and it licked up the water that was in the trench. Now when all the people saw it, they fell on their faces; and they said, "The Lord, He is God! The Lord, He is God!" (1 Kings 18:36-39)

I truly feel compassion for those who are wrestling with the great questions of life, especially those dealing with the question of the existence of God. Not everyone was raised in a Christian home where faith in God was so woven into their worldview that it became an intricate part of their mental makeup and belief system. On the contrary, many have been raised in an environment where answers were sought from a purely academic or rational point of view, which naturally led them to science, which by its very methodological processes excludes the possibility of the transcendent altogether. They are taught that what cannot be discovered through empirical means simply cannot be a part of the discussion in regard to seeking answers to the mysteries of the universe. They see talk about God as a cop out; a lazy way of attributing what we don't understand to some "higher power."

In fact, I have heard the argument that each time science uncovers another mystery that can be explained through natural processes, it lessens the room that can be found for God. This is what's known as "the God of the gaps." In other words, as the gaps in our knowledge are filled with understanding of the natural processes of the universe, God is displaced. For example, they will say that once upon a time man thought that lighting was the result of the anger of the gods. People trembled and revered the gods and paid them homage, lest they should suffer the retribution of the angered deities. Of course, since we now know that lightning is the result of purely natural processes, we've eliminated one more place for God to hide. Soon, atheistic scientists assume, all the remaining mysteries will be discovered, or at least sufficient of them, to prove that there is no God hiding behind anything anywhere, and that He does not, in fact, exist.

The truth is, I don't have enough faith to be an atheist. The discoveries of science in more recent years have uncovered the tremendous complexities of the cell. What was once considered the "simple" cell has been proven to be anything but! In fact, the systems in a single cell are so intricate and complex that it's beyond any rational possibility for the materialist to explain through the unguided, natural processes of Darwinism. The DNA molecule is a complex information repository with over three billion bits of information in the form of a four-letter chemical alphabet, like a digital code, arranged in a specific sequence so as to instruct amino acids how to link together to form the proper protein molecules that in turn comprise the different structures in our bodies. What no one seems to be able to answer, from a materialist's standpoint, is how natural selection, acting on random variations, created such a complex communication system. Who provided the programing, and furthermore, how does the cell know how to "read" and utilize the information contained therein?

The point is that wherever you have information, you have intelligence, because the characters only have meaning because that meaning is assigned to them by some intelligent agent outside the system, such as a computer programmer who creates the code which gives instruction to the computer. On a much simpler level, if you and I were to happen upon a beach that had a message written in the sand saying, "Hello, I hope you have a wonderful day," would we for one moment believe that those words appeared by chance through natural processes over billions of years? No! We would immediately infer intelligence. Yet this message I have suggested on the beach is but a trifle when compared to the incredibly complex, coded message of the DNA molecule, which is contained in each one of the one-hundred-trillion cells in our bodies.

Sir Fred Hoyle, a brilliant cosmologist, explained the impossibility of life beginning on earth through naturalistic processes by saying, *"Biochemical systems are exceedingly complex, so much so that the chance of their being formed through random shuffling of simple organic molecules is exceedingly minute, to a point where it is no different from zero... For life to have originated on earth it would be necessary that quite explicit instructions should have been provided for its assembly.*"[2]

Nobel Prize Laureate, Sir Francis Crick, who discovered the double-helical structure of DNA, said, *"An honest man, armed with all the knowledge available to us now, could only state that in some sense, the origin of life appears at the moment to be almost a miracle, so many are the conditions which would have had to have been satisfied to get it going."* [3]

Hoyle adds, *"The trouble is that there are about two thousand enzymes, and the chance of obtaining them all in a random trial is only one part in $(10^{20})2,000=10^{40,000}$, an outrageously small probability that could not be faced even if the whole universe consisted of organic soup."*[4]

These are not theists or a Christians postulating about the improbability of life starting from naturalistic means. These are atheists and scientists with enough honesty to say that this simply did not happen by chance. When pressed further, however, to explain what he did believe was the mechanism that started life, Crick fell back on the impossibly ridiculous theory of *panspermia*, which is to say that an extraterrestrial civilization from another solar system "seeded" our planet with the necessary ingredients to form life. So, essentially, we're here because ET jettisoned his space junk in a puddle of goo here on earth (folks, I can't even make this stuff up). Hoyle expressed the same belief, keeping the explanation as far away as possible from the God of the Bible.

Of course, this doesn't answer the obvious question, "Who made the aliens that seeded our planet?" Assuming they also exist, one still must answer the problem of the impossibility of life forming by chance (even if it happened on Vulcan). So Hoyle postulates that there must indeed be a Supreme Being out there whom these aliens serve by performing this task of spreading life throughout the cosmos. He further says that since it is they who serve Him and not us, we are under no obligation to this Higher Being. That's a pretty fantastic story to create just to avoid accountability to God.

Listen, I like Star Trek as much as the next mad scientist, but seriously? This is not a bunch of crazies waiting in line to attend the next Comic Con. These are Nobel prize-winning scientists and their peers struggling to answer how such complex life came into existence from non-living material in the first place. From a materialist's point of view, such seemingly complex life somehow came into existence without the benefit of a designer by undirected, natural processes. What Hoyle and Crick are saying is that this is beyond the realm of possibility. In fact, the chances of even a single "simple" protein molecule assembling by random, evolutionary processes over time is 1 in 10^{125}, a probability so incredibly remote it is simply beyond all reasonable question. Were it not for the fact that the plain answer to the origin of life held such enormous moral implications, there would be no dispute, for wherever we find design, and even more particularly, information, we naturally infer intelligence. Thus, these incredibly complex, living systems are crying out like the proverbial rocks of which Jesus spoke, that God is the Creator, the very One whom our white robed friends are trying so desperately to keep from getting a foot in the door!

I have shared this to present a scientific basis for belief for those who do not accept the authority of the biblical text as proof of God's existence. However, for me and for millions who *do* believe in God, these discoveries are merely the predictable backdrop of a Christian worldview that already presupposes the existence of God. To me it seems clear that the prophetic fulfillments of scripture, the life, death, and resurrection of Jesus, not to mention the impact He has singularly made on the course of human history, is sufficient evidence for solid faith. We can declare that not only is there a God, but that He came to earth as one of us. Yes, life indeed came from an extraterrestrial source. The Bible tells us as much.

In the beginning was the Word, and the Word was with God, and the Word was God. He was in the beginning with God. All things were made through Him, and without Him nothing was made that was made (John 1:1-3).

Not only did Jesus, the Living Word, create the Universe, He got personally involved with you and I when He came to earth as a man, born of a virgin, to take our sins upon Himself and die on our behalf, thus balancing the scales of divine justice and redeeming us back to God. This same Jesus God raised from the dead in an act of power no less tremendous than when He spoke the worlds into being. He is alive, and as living God, still makes the lightning in the sky. He is the Creator and superintending, sustaining Agent of the universe. He is God Most High, to whom every knee will bow and every tongue confess that He is Lord (see Philippians 2:5-11).

In Elijah's day, that fire fell from the sky and consumed the sacrifice on Mount Carmel, bringing an entire backslidden nation to God. In my own life and ministry, I have seen the power of God heal the sick and restore joy to the barren womb. I have seen the incurably sick receive word that their disease miraculously disappeared, and I have seen those oppressed, in the very literal grip of the devil, instantly set free through the anointing and power of the Holy Spirit.

I could show you dozens of testimonies from the nation of India that tell of a Jesus who revealed Himself alive to men and women of a different faith altogether, healing their bodies and even restoring to wholeness those who had been developmentally disabled.

My favorite testimony is from a humble Indian family whose young daughter, Jasmine, was admitted to the hospital with brain fever. She was in agony, despite the good doctors' best efforts to relieve her suffering. Because they were regular viewers of our television broadcast, they went home and took some recorded healing messages to play at the hospital to strengthen their faith. As they played the videos and prayed in faith, their daughter was raised up and began praising God. They shared how, not only she, but the patients in the two adjacent rooms were also healed by the simple power of the gospel.

How is this possible? Because our God is the God who answers by fire. He is the eternal, transcendent First Cause of the Universe who bent so low as to completely identify with us at our lowest and take upon Himself the sins of the world. Having secured our deliverance, He stands ready to save all who will simply believe and call upon His name.

No friends, my faith is not in an alien civilization on some distant planet, but in the God who makes His home in the heart of the redeemed. If you will call upon Him, even to simply ask Him to make Himself real to you, His lightning will flash once more from heaven to illuminate your heart to the reality of the living God. If you are truly looking for reality and want to understand the greater mysteries, go to the One who is the true source of it all. He is real, He is love, and He is waiting to reveal Himself to you.

PURSUIT OF APPROVAL

When He had been baptized, Jesus came up immediately from the water; and behold, the heavens were opened to Him, and He saw the Spirit of God descending like a dove and alighting upon Him. And suddenly a voice came from heaven, saying, "This is My beloved Son, in whom I am well pleased. (Matthew 3:16-17)

When it comes to looking at healthy family relationships, I don't think we can do better than to look at the mystical union that exists within the Trinity: Father, Son, and Holy Spirit. With our finite understanding we can never perhaps begin to comprehend the union and unity that exists among the three distinct Persons of the Godhead, but what we can trace throughout scripture is the love and honor which God the Father and Jesus demonstrated toward one another during Christ's earthly ministry. Jesus constantly gave honor to the Father, always crediting Him with His very words and works, always seeking to please Him and do His will. On more than one occasion the Father Himself spoke audibly from Heaven to honor the Son, who submitted Himself so completely to the Father's will.

While it is safe to say that Jesus did not suffer from insecurity, He did know what it was to feel the Father's rejection, as He became sin's sacrifice on the cross. There He cried, "My God, My God, why have You forsaken Me?" (Matthew 27:46). He was not rejected for His own deeds, but suffered shame and isolation from the Father on our behalf, that we might be reconciled unto God. Also, I think it significant that in the very first temptation in which we see the devil approach Christ in the wilderness, he attempted to cast the shadow of doubt regarding the Son's relationship with his Father. "Now when the tempter came to Him, he said, '*If You are the Son of God*, command that these stones become bread'" (Matthew 4:3). Such a wonderful source of strength was the Son's awareness of His Father's approval that the devil sought, however he might, to undermine Christ's sense of it, all to no avail.

Christ's confidence and boldness came not only from knowing Who He was, but also from knowing that He was always operating within the parameters of His Father's approval. I think we can see something of a pattern of God's intent here, that Christ's public ministry began with this very public demonstration of His Father's approval. In fact, there was never a time, save for that moment of separation on the cross, when Jesus was not keenly aware of His Father's regard, unlike many in the world today who have never felt such approval from their own fathers, despite their best efforts to impress. Millions today suffer from the severe affliction of simply never feeling that they had the love, support, and approval from a father or a mother.

In fact, I believe the pursuit of approval is one of mans' most pervasive pursuits. It is an unbidden guide by which many unwittingly steer their life. Seeking from someone, anyone, the approval that God initially intended us to experience in the comfort and security of parental delight, and ultimately from Him, as we find unconditional love and acceptance through a relationship with Jesus Christ. Regardless of what men may say, we all, to one degree or another, pursue the approval of someone. The celebrity seeks it from his adoring fans, while the sports hero finds it in the adulation of the roaring crowd. The ambitious son endeavors to outstrip his successful father, while every little boy who plays in little league looks to see the expression on his parents' face, whether he hits a home run or drops the fly ball in center field.

Sometimes the drive to find acceptance fuels a manic energy that keeps one ever moving, ever climbing, desirous to succeed in the eyes of those whose praise matters most to them. As children we have our heroes whom we see as deserving of praise and think that if we could ever be like them we would have the love and adoration we so desperately seek. Sometimes this drive for approval is expressed in contrary ways, such as in the case of the runaway teen that continues to get into trouble with the authorities, a not-so-silent cry for someone to take notice and intervene, to tell them that they are loved, valued, and significant.

We all want to feel it, that sense of worth, and many have dashed themselves against the ruined rocks of addiction and hopeless frustration in their vain pursuit for it. The broken cisterns from which desperate men seek to slake their thirst multiply in our society as they move from one vise to the next, looking for anything that will fit and fill the aching void inside. We want to feel singularly significant to someone, yet all the while the failed nature of mankind has taught us that we are expendable rather than valuable, even to the people who are supposed to matter most. Marriages fail, trust between child and parent is broken, and the best of friends betray us with a kiss, leveraging their connection with us merely to advance their own ends. Where in this world can we find that one who will love us for ourselves alone?

Such a love is not to be found *in this world*. Rather, it is offered to the entire world by the God Who created us and put His claim upon us long ago. Before the foundations of the world He decided our purchase price was greater than all the gold and silver in all the coffers of all the kingdoms of this world. He set the price of our redemption at the high cost of His only begotten Son, who willingly laid down His life for us, the innocent for the guilty, the lovely for the unlovely. What makes this love special is that it is guileless and true, not based on a false sense of who we are, but with perfect understanding of our faults and foibles. He took us as we were because He determines our value to be great. He saw past the trash to the treasure. Though we were sinners, He made a way to bridge the gap and close the distance between us so that we would not be standing outside the gates of His grace like beggars, but welcomed into His house as sons and daughters.

This is favor too great to earn, too costly to merit. It can only be received as a gift. One must simply do honor to the Giver of gifts and receive by faith the proffered prize of acceptance in the Beloved. This is a gift purchased by wealth too great for this world, but extended to us all that we might be lifted up and seated at the Father's table. Nor is this newfound belonging only for the life that is to come. Our new identity in Christ gives us a welcomed place in His family here and now as well, for as the psalmist says, "God places the lonely in families; He sets the prisoners free and gives them joy" (Psalm 68:6 *NLT*). If you have searched your whole life long for this love and approval, search no further. It is found in the person of Jesus. Welcome home.

THE ROAD AHEAD

Just think how much more the blood of Christ will purify our consciences from sinful deeds so that we can worship the living God. For by the power of the eternal Spirit, Christ offered himself to God as a perfect sacrifice for our sins. (Hebrews 9:14 *New Living Translation*)

Normally, the rear view mirror reflects those things that are behind us, which grow more and more distant and indistinct as we continue to move forward toward our destination. Even large objects that might take up the entire field of vision in that mirror soon diminish and ultimately fade from view as we move forward and continue on our journey. We can learn a lot from a good rear view mirror.

Some people, even Christians, have a hard time letting certain things fade into the background of their lives and disappear. A rear view mirror is uniquely positioned to keep the image of what is behind us still before our eyes, even while we are endeavoring to look forward to where we're going. Likewise, a guilty conscience may cause one to keep past sins and mistakes in view, clouding the vision of tomorrow with an image of yesterday's failure.

Some, who refuse to pry their eyes away from that image of what's behind them, can lose site of the road that's before them altogether, allowing condemnation to reverse their direction, as they revisit the moment of their failure again and again. They may feel stuck, unable to put their life "in drive" again until they *feel* forgiven, choosing to let feelings and emotions of guilt control them, rather than faith in God's Word, which tells us we are forgiven the moment we acknowledge our sin to God (see 1 John 1:9). The Bible is clear that we walk by faith and not by sight, and sometimes the only way to put distance between us and our past is to simply put our life in gear again. As we choose to move forward by faith, the disparity between faith and feeling is bridged and the healing of our heart can begin.

Christ's blood was shed to clear the reflection of yesterday's wrongdoing that stains our wounded conscience. Only the blood of Christ has power to remove the dark mark of sin upon the soul, restore our heart, and make it whole. God does not want us trying to pay for our sins on the installment plan, regularly revisiting our failure and reliving the shame. No, Christ paid it all, and the only way to do honor to His sacrifice is to realize that it was made to release us from all shame, that the imprint of sin on our conscience may be completely removed.

So, put some distance between you and your yesterdays. The sooner you start moving forward again, the sooner the objects in your mirror will be replaced with a new view. Your feelings will soon catch up with your faith, the wounds of your conscience will heal, and your confidence in His purpose for your life will be restored.

After all, the same Peter who denied Christ on the eve of his crucifixion was the Peter who saw three thousand souls come to faith on the day of Pentecost, less than two months later. The Moses who killed the Egyptian and became a fugitive on the backside of the desert was the very same Moses who became the wonder-working deliver of God's covenant people. The same David who failed morally was the king whom God called, "A man after My own heart." The vision of your past failures can truly be replaced by a bright expectation for tomorrow, and your best days can honestly be just down the road ahead.

COMPETENT IN YOUR CONTEXT

And He has made from one blood every nation of men to dwell on all the face of the earth, and has determined their preappointed times and the boundaries of their dwellings, so that they should seek the Lord, in the hope that they might grope for Him and find Him, though He is not far from each one of us. (Acts 17:26-27)

God is the One who determined your context; the environment, culture, and even the time into which you were born. He put you when and where He did so that you might seek Him and find Him. Some of us might question whether the particular condition into which we were born was really the best for our spiritual search, but God knows what we do not. His placement of you was significant to His purposes for your life.

Context plays an enormous role in influencing our lives. It does much to determine who we become and how our lives and values will be shaped. For example, the writer of the Proverbs said, "He who walks with wise men will be wise, but the companion of fools will be destroyed" (Proverbs 13:20). Paul said something similar when he said, "Do not be deceived: 'Evil company corrupts good habits'"

(1 Corinthians 15:33). The people who influence us as we develop are a huge part of the context that shapes us. We will rise or fall to the level of our associations. If we are raised in an environment of intellectual curiosity, we will most likely grow up asking questions, reading widely, and being interested in new people and new places. If we were raised in a community without much outside influence, we might grow up suspicious of viewpoints or perspectives that step outside the boundaries of what was the conventional wisdom of those who influenced us most.

Paul, being a citizen of Rome, a very cosmopolitan city, as well as being a well-traveled and educated man, found it easier than some might to identify with a wide range of people. He speaks of his efforts to find points of connection with those he encountered so that he might find an avenue for the gospel. He said, "…to the Jews I became as a Jew, that I might win Jews; to those who are under the law, as under the law, that I might win those who are under the law; to those who are without law, as without law (not being without law toward God, but under law toward Christ), that I might win those who are without law; to the weak I became as weak, that I might win the weak. I have become all things to all men, that I might by all means save some. Now this I do for the gospel's sake…" (1 Corinthians 9:20-23).

Paul was not being disingenuous when he behaved like a chameleon, conforming his communication efforts to match the culture he was addressing. He was merely being relevant. We've all probably found those to whom we simply could not connect. Maybe they were from a different part of the world or from a very different culture or ethnicity with which we had little affinity. We are all different, and while it's good to try to gain an understanding of other people and their worldview or way of life, we will always feel more at home among those most like us. This is not necessarily a bad thing. After all, God is the one who made the determination of when and where you would be born and by what culture you would be shaped. This is the very reason that missionaries spend more time training indigenous believers to reach their own people than trying to do all the evangelizing themselves. They've learned that those who already know the language, culture, and are at home in their surroundings, make the best missionaries.

This in no way is to discourage any of us from trying to gain a better understanding of people from other places who think and believe very differently from us. On the contrary, with the global community getting smaller every day by virtue of our connectivity through technology, it is more important than ever to be culturally sensitive to people who come from a very different context than our own. However, we should also realize that, like any other indigenous missionary, you have great potential for influence in the place where God planted you.

My mother, who was an enormous influence on my own spiritual life, used to get frustrated with people that thought they had to go somewhere other than their own hometown to be used by God. There is often an assumption that if we are going to find our place in the world, it has to be somewhere other than where we were born and shaped. I am saying, "Not so." Some of us had to go away and see much of the world outside before we could truly appreciate the folks back home.

God planted you where He did for His purpose, and He allowed you to be shaped by the culture and context into which He placed you that you might be uniquely equipped to identify with those around you and communicate the gospel effectively. Even Jesus was born a Jew that He might first reach out to God's covenant people. His dress, language and mannerisms would have been profoundly Jewish, enabling Him to better reach the people to whom he was sent (see Matthew 15:24).

Now we, the worldwide body of Christ, are everywhere, in every context, that we might together reach the world for Christ. You may very well find yourself serving God in a very different place from where you started, but if not, realize that God kept you close to your roots to reach those who share that special heritage with you.

GOD AT WORK

Therefore, my beloved, as you have always obeyed, not as in my presence only, but now much more in my absence, work out your own salvation with fear and trembling; for it is God who works in you both to will and to do for His good pleasure. (Philippians 2:12)

Some years back while pastoring in New England, a couple moved to our state to be a part of our church. God put it in their heart to come, and we were delighted to have them as a part of our church family. They were Bible school graduates, and they both served in our church for a number of years, occupying leadership roles.

However, as happened with a number of people who were new to the Northeast, the adjustment was not without difficulty. The difference in climate, culture, and being away from family, made the transition tough for a while. I would see it particularly in the wife, whose eyes were often filled with tears during service, and I knew her faith was being tested. I also knew it was likely that she, if not both of them, were perhaps second-guessing themselves and their decision.

The husband's struggle was in his ability to find work in the printing industry, which was already suffering from the innovation of desktop publishing. There were simply no jobs around like he had had before, and something else would have to be found to meet the family budget. Eventually he did find work, though it was hard, physical labor, probably more suited for a younger man than for one middle-aged.

I felt for them. I had seen others likewise struggle, and as their pastor I wanted to step in and do all I could to make the transition less difficult. I tend to be a pretty mercy-motivated individual, not liking to see anyone face a challenge or go through hardship, let alone those of my own congregation for whom I feel some responsibility. However, God taught me a valuable lesson in dealing with people through this experience. He very definitely told me to step back and allow Him to finish what He had begun in them. God let me know that what I thought was stepping in to help was really interfering with His process in their lives.

Sometimes we just have to realize that we are not God. We are not the Savior, and sometimes when stepping in to make someone else's process easier, we inadvertently undermine a work of God in their lives. Maturing is not always easy, and there are some lessons regarding faith and patience, character development, and spiritual growth that we can learn no other way than to simply go through them. We've all seen what happens when parents won't let their children grow up, stepping into every conflict on their behalf to right the world's wrongs. Those children often grow up incapable of handling anything on their own, shouting to all who will hear that the world is unfair anytime circumstances don't fall their way.

There are times when, no matter how much we want to help, we need to realize that God is at work, and the only way some victories can come, some lessons can be learned, and some maturing take place in people's lives, is to let them work it out between themselves and God. No two people's journey of faith is the same, and sometimes we can give poor advice, telling others what we think they should do, when really they need to be going to God rather than to us.

This is a lesson I have had to learn on a number of occasions in my own life as well, when certain spiritual victories could not be won through another's prayers or by letting others fight my battles for me. Sometimes we have to fight the giant ourselves, and when we win, we have a testimony of God's faithfulness that is our own and not another's. It is the accumulation of these hard-fought victories, where God and God alone brought us out, that give us wisdom and experience that can speak into the lives of others when it is appropriate to do so. This is the way maturity comes.

Some time back, my wife and I started an outreach in wine country. As we toured the vineyards, I noticed there seemed to be little by way of irrigation. I asked the tour guide why this was, and she said something to this effect: "It's the struggle of the vine that gives it its flavor." Wow. What a message! Again and again, Jesus tells us through John that the rewards are to the "overcomers" (see Revelation, chapters 2 & 3), and there are some battles we are simply going to have to fight until we win. God will be with us, but He's not going to do it all for us. He expects us to use our faith, exercise patience, practice perseverance, and stay the course, faithfully obeying Him. That's how it's done. That's how disciples are made. That's how God works in us to make us the men and women He's called us to be.

PEOPLE

Jesus called his disciples to him and said, "I have compassion for these people…" (Matthew 15:32)

People: just the word inspires different thoughts and feelings in each of us. Sometimes we see the ridiculous things of which people are capable and we lift our eyebrows, shake our heads, and say, "People!" Other times we see the images of the teeming masses of humanity in impoverished, famine stricken nations, and it takes our breath as we think of all the hurting people.

At some time or another, we have all been so sick of people, whether it was family members we fought with, backstabbing coworkers who used us to their advantage, or the inconsiderate people caught up in the busy hustle and bustle of life, taking our parking place, crowding ahead of us in line, or flipping us off, even though they were the ones who cut us off in traffic. Yes, we all have those moments when we'd just like to get away from all the people.

If it's any consolation, Jesus had his troubles with people too, and not just the obvious ones either! Jesus struggled against pharisaical, religious hypocrites, of course, but He also had challenges with His ministry staff and even His own family. The former clamored for position while the latter thought that He had taken leave of His senses. People.

John's Gospel tells us that Jesus knew He couldn't entrust Himself to the adoring crowds that followed Him and beheld His miracles because He knew what people were capable of deep down (see John 2:23-25). He was right, and in the end the same crowds that had at one time lauded Him as God's anointed man of the hour, were the same people who were stirred up to cry, "Crucify Him!" In fact, it was one of the people closest to Him that placed the kiss of betrayal upon His cheek.

For all of that God still loves people. In fact, the Bible clearly tells us that "God so loved *all the people* that he gave his one and only Son, that whoever believes in him shall not perish but have eternal life." (John 3:16 *author's paraphrase*). It should say something to us that the One who knows people the best still believes in us enough to make such sacrifice on our behalf.

When you see people, do you see the problem or the potential? Before you think you know the right answer, you need to realize that people come with both! You and I know that because we are people too. You can't mine a person's potential without having to deal with the problems that come with people. Some of the greatest relationships I've had, that taught me the most, also came with the greatest problems. Sometimes the kid you raised that gave you the most grief, ends up becoming the greatest achiever, as he or she begins to realize his or her potential.

All of us can be a problem. All of us have great potential. If the cross shows us anything, it shows us that people are worth the investment. Every relationship you will ever have will have problems, but the people God brings into your life have a potential to help you realize *your* potential and bring things out of you that you never dreamed possible. So, love people regardless of the problem they can be. That's not to say that we shouldn't be wise and discerning as to whom we let into our innermost councils or the secret places of our heart. Even Jesus chose His disciples after spending all night in prayer. But we are to love people, realizing that God put us all in the people business, and that in every person born into this world there is great potential beyond the problem.

CRISIS OF COMMITMENT

Simon Peter said to Him, "Lord, where are You going?" Jesus answered him, "Where I am going you cannot follow Me now, but you shall follow Me afterward." Peter said to Him, "Lord, why can I not follow You now? I will lay down my life for Your sake." Jesus answered him, "Will you lay down your life for My sake? Most assuredly, I say to you, the rooster shall not crow till you have denied Me three times." (John 13:36-38)

In this brief exchange between Jesus and Peter, I think we can recognize an issue of superficiality that exists in the lives of many believers today. I do not believe that Peter was being disingenuous when he declared his willingness to die for the Master so much as he was overestimating the level of his commitment. On the one side, Peter had left his trade and all that he knew to follow Jesus, and later when the moment of Judas' betrayal came, Peter demonstrated his willingness to stand at his Master's side when he struck the servant of the high priest, cutting off his ear. However, when Jesus healed the man, telling Peter to put away his sword, the dynamic seemed to change. Though he had warned the disciples of His impending crucifixion in the days preceding the event, I'm not so sure that it wasn't until this moment that they really realized that their assumptions about the Messiah's mission were wrong. He was not going to put down Roman rule and restore the Kingdom to Israel as they had assumed days before when they were debating on the road who among them would be first in the Kingdom, seated on His right and on His left.

Peter's resolve to stand at his Master's side evaporated along with his false assumptions about the Messiah's mission as "all the disciples forsook Him and fled" in that desperate moment in the garden (see Matthew 25:47-56). Most of us know the story of how Peter followed at a distance to see what the fate of His Lord would be. These men had cast in their lot with this miracle working teacher, forsaking everything to follow Him and have a stake in the Kingdom He would establish, and now, as the events of the night and following day unfolded, their world seemed to crumble before their eyes as they witnessed the unthinkable. As far as they were concerned, their dreams died with Jesus on that cross, and their hopes were buried with Him in the tomb. Peter finished the night in bitter weeping, having fulfilled the Messiah's prediction that he would deny he ever knew Him.

All of us have played the role of armchair quarterback in life, I'm sure. Sometimes we do so literally, as we watch our favorite team make mistakes on the field that we can easily identify from the comfort and safety of our recliner, with no large, heavily-limbed linebackers ready to crush the life out of us if we fail to accurately read the defense quickly enough. It's easy to see from a safe vantage point, away from the heat of battle, or even in retrospect, what others should have done in their crisis moment. We might even conclude our critique of their performance by presumptively asserting to ourselves that we would have done things differently. We would have done better.

That's what Peter had thought. He even stated it in the very presence of the other disciples. "Peter said to Him, 'Even if all are made to stumble, yet I will not be'" (Mark 14:29). However, as we know from the story, Peter did not stand the test. He denied the Lord, and was not present, as John was, at the foot of the cross as Jesus breathed his last. However, I am certain that Peter had no less love for the Master than any of the others who followed Him. His genuine repentance, subsequent restoration by the resurrected Christ, life of service, and ultimate martyr's death, prove that Peter indeed rose to make the ultimate sacrifice for the Lord he loved.

Like Peter, we can all become more than we are. God is not done with any of us, so there's hope, even for those of us who think our commitment is made of sterner stuff than it is. I can't speak for you, but I disappoint myself sometimes in my commitment and walk with the Lord. It seems that while I want to speak great swelling words of self-sacrifice, like Peter did, I too seem to struggle with what should be the more basic issues of commitment. Daily disobediences belie the words of dedication I may speak in those "all on the altar" moments in church. Love for mundane, worldly pleasures can rob me of my appetite for spiritual things, causing my Bible to spend too many lonely hours without my attention, or cause my prayer life to suffer. I allow in the "little" sins, the evidence of my tattered commitment, then confess them and pledge to do better, giving God a quick "high five" because He's so good, without appreciating the fact that His grace and forgiveness are only available because of the unspeakable tortures the spotless Son of God suffered on my behalf.

We can talk some good talk, but before we start saying we'll go the distance, we should really stop and ask ourselves where we are in the present. If we're not committed to the most basic of biblical demands; paying our tithes, being faithful to the house of God, living separated, holy lives, and denying fleshly lusts, for example, will we really make the ultimate sacrifice? No, we won't, because we're not. If we're not faithful with that which is least, we will certainly not do better when truly great demand is placed upon our undeveloped spiritual muscles. The very fact we haven't faced some temptations may be because God is faithful not to allow us to be tempted above what we are able (see 1 Corinthians 10:13), so we can forget about condemning the brother or sister that fell from heights we can't even see from where we stand.

This is not meant to be a harsh criticism of other believers. We all share the same liabilities and must overcome the same inherent weakness of the flesh. However, I do think that we in North America in general, and the United States in particular, need a wakeup call to the prerequisites of discipleship. It would seem that believers today are like modern furniture: not made of the same stuff they used to be. I love the stories of men like C.T. Studd, who gave up a lucrative career as an English cricketer to become a missionary to China, and later established the Heart of Africa Mission, which later became the Worldwide Evangelistic Crusade (now WEC International). He penned the now famous poem that contains the verse, "Only one life, 'twill soon be past. Only what's done for Christ will last." He gave his inheritance of £29,000 away to the work of God, believing God would meet his needs as he served Him. He famously said, "Some want to live within the sound of church or chapel bell; I want to run a rescue shop within a yard of hell."

His is just one story in the vast procession of men and women of true faith who paid a great price to advance the cause of Christ, some of whom gave their very lives; men and women of whom the world was not worthy. The work of these true disciples, like that of the early disciples, continues on, still producing fruit that remains until the present day. It is from these men that the Church must learn today, taking a page from the book of their devotion: men whose lives, as well as their deaths, expressed a commitment that was not coerced or forced, but given freely as the only fitting offering to the Lord Who had given His all to redeem them.

It is possible that some of us in this part of the world will be asked to pay with our lives as Peter ultimately did. But more importantly, we must rise to the challenge to truly *give* our lives, each and every day, in faithful service the One we call Lord. I have fallen short, as have perhaps some of you, but I am encouraged by Peter. His story started with big words and poor deeds, but finished with deeds for which no words are adequate. We too can become more than we are at the present time. The Lord still knows how to take the raw timber of our humble surrender and build a disciple whose foundations go down to the very rock of His Word and whose light can shine out across the troubles seas of this world to lead men safely home.

THE MEETING ON
STRAIGHT STREET

Now there was a certain disciple at Damascus named Ananias;
and to him the Lord said in a vision, "Ananias." And he said,
"Here I am, Lord." So the Lord said to him, "Arise and go to the
street called Straight, and inquire at the house of Judas for one
called Saul of Tarsus, for behold, he is praying. And in a vision
he has seen a man named Ananias coming in and putting his
hand on him, so that he might receive his sight." (Acts 9:10-12)

The gospel is good news. That being the case, it is strange that
so many Christians are convinced that no one wants to hear
it. It is safe to say that many professing believers will go their whole
lives without purposely sharing their faith. If indeed we believe, as
the Bible teaches, that those who fail to believe in Christ are doomed
to eternal separation from the presence of God in a place of torment,
why in the world would be keep quiet about such an important message as the death, burial, and resurrection of Christ? We don't want
to be a bother?

Most of us are probably sensitive to the fact that many people
outside the Church feel that Christians can tend to be "pushy" about

their faith at times, and perhaps we've all met that tactless believer whose opening witnessing line tends to be something about "burning in hell if you don't repent." Granted, there is a right and a wrong way to do it, but we cannot escape the fact that all of us who have been saved by the grace of God have also been commissioned to share our faith with others. In fact, the Church has been tasked by God with making disciples in all the nations of the world (see Matthew 28:18-20). Not only that, but Jesus promised He would be with us in the Person of the Holy Spirit to help and to empower us to be effective witnesses for Him (see Acts 1:8).

Perhaps we all know people whom we desperately want to see come to faith, who, for one reason or another, simply seem to be hardened to the message of the gospel. If ever there was such a person, it was Saul of Tarsus. His fierce persecution against the Church stemmed from an over-zealous determination to see what he deemed to be an up-start religious cult stamped out as quickly and thoroughly as possible. It was for that very reason that he had headed to Damascus in the first place—to extend his efforts to eradicate the Church wherever She was found. Saul's mission had not gone unnoticed by the Church, either. When the Lord appeared to Ananias to send him to minister to the world's most notorious religious zealot, Ananias initially objected. "Then Ananias answered, 'Lord, I have heard from many about this man, how much harm he has done to Your saints in Jerusalem. And here he has authority from the chief priests to bind all who call on Your name.'" (Acts 9:13-14).

What Ananias could not have known is that the Lord had already met with Saul in what is without a doubt the most famous conversion recorded in scripture. It was on the Damascus road that Jesus had already softened up the spirited Pharisee, and all Ananias would have to do is deliver the knock-out punch. When he arrived at the house on Straight Street, he did not find a hate-filled, death-dealing terrorist, as he had expected, but a greatly humbled, broken man, ready to respond to the grace of God. God had gone before Ananias and done all the heavy lifting.

In reality, God always does all the heavy lifting. Neither you or I can bring a soul to Christ. We do our part: we share our faith, demonstrate the love and character of Christ to a lost world, but in the end, it's God who draws the sinner home (see John 6:65). What we as believers need to see is that we're not in this alone. Jesus said He would be with us until the end of the age (see Matthew 28:20), and He has given us His Spirit as an ever-present Helper (see John 14:16). God goes with us, working on the hearts of those who hear the good news as we share, convincing, persuading, and softening the listener's heart, so that the seed of the Word might produce a harvest of eternal life.

Sometimes, God has gone ahead long before us, preparing the way so that the message of the gospel is like fresh rain on a wilted plant, thirsty for life, or a like a life preserver thrown to a man drowning in the deep waters of his own sin-wrecked life. Too often, we count out the very one whose former passion against the truth makes them an ardent defender of the faith once their convictions are turned toward God. Saul, the most unlikely candidate for Christianity, became Paul the apostle, the most famous Christian of all time, whose impact on the world is still felt each time a Bible is given or purchased or the faith is shared from the epistles he authored.

We all, like Ananias, are called and commissioned to share the good news, both to the hungry and the stubborn soul. It is not for us to assume that anyone is too hardened to receive the good news. Their noisy objections may only be a thin façade; a flimsy defense mechanism easily washed away in the tidal wave of God's grace. Never underestimate the persuasive power of the Holy Spirit, nor the power of the truth, breaking like warm light in a cold, darkened heart. God wants the world to know His salvation. So much so, He invested Heaven's very best to secure that redemption for every man, woman, boy and girl, in every nation, for all time. God has given us the privilege of partnering with Him in this great soul-saving work. All we have to do is obey. He's already done the hard part.

CHANGE OF SEASON

To everything there is a season,

A time for every purpose under heaven. (Ecclesiastes 3:1)

Fall is approaching. I love the autumn season. It has always been far and away my favorite time of year. I loved it in New England when the changing colors of the leaves would set the woods ablaze with their endless variety of greens, reds and yellows. I love the smell of the early Fall mornings which always take me back to memories of the first days of the new school year growing up. I love everything about the Fall season, except that it doesn't last. No season does. They come and they go. I used to tease the Vermonters I lived around for years that they never advertise that those beautiful colors only last a few weeks before the entire region is plunged into a six-month winter! That part was never in the brochures.

Life is a succession of seasons. I'm sure I heard that at some point in my life, but it has only been as I've gotten older that I've seen just how true it is. So many of the expectations of youth are undermined by what we come to realize later in life; that many things simply don't last. They are only here for a season. The friendships, the career, and the house we now live in; all these things will likely be different at another stage of life. Some of the people who play a significant role in your life today will likely become a fond memory you treasure a little further down the road. We mean to keep in touch, but in reality, things change.

I remember talking to a church member of mine once who was telling me with tears that he was transferring to a different university to be a researcher there. He had to leave now, but he would be back. I smiled and said that would be great. He never came back. I knew it was unlikely that he ever would. That's just life. Some of the changes we experience are welcome. Others come with serious misgivings. But change will come. This realization has affected the way I approach life. When a new ministry assignment comes, I dive into it with the commitment to last a lifetime, but I know now that it very well may have an expiration date attached. I give myself wholly to what God has set before me, but I have too often had that encounter with the changing seasons in life to become surprised when God begins to stir within me a new direction for life and service

When people come into my world, I now realize that while we may very well be connected for life, there is that possibility that God has put us in one another's path for a season and for a reason. It may be that they need something I can impart to them for the next stage of their journey. It may be that such a relationship will teach me something about people and their struggles that I will take with me for the rest of my life and find invaluable in helping others with similar struggles. They may serve as a mentor to help prepare me for events that will take place in the upcoming season of my life. A few people have remained in my life through every season, and they are the ones that know me better than I know myself. They are the ones I may not see every day, month, or even year, but when we do reconnect, it is as though no time has passed since the last time we were together. We pick right back up where we left off.

For myself, I have accepted that the change of seasons we encounter are like chapters in the story that God is writing of our life. It is normal and healthy that we part from one season and move to the next with a touch of sadness, as we will miss the people and places attached to that part of our journey, but we should never despair as though our whole life was meant to be defined by that passing season. I have to admit, that often it was in the more difficult seasons that I grew the most. I may not have liked it at the time, but it was necessary to mature and prepare me for what God had in the seasons to follow. God is a good guide, and He is ever taking us deeper into His best for our lives.

I have also seen, in my particular case (maybe you have seen this too), that God was not necessarily responsible for every season I had to go through in life. My own poor choices landed me in some places that God in His omniscience saw coming, and by His grace, He sustained me through it. I know what it is to feel like an exile in a strange land, due to no one's fault but my own, and yet, I can honestly say that I have never experienced the love and grace of God in a greater way than when He was patiently lifting me out of that pit of my own digging. That's grace; God giving us His best when we are not at ours.

Ultimately, if we have faith to put our life in His hands, we will look back and see that He has artfully navigated us in and out of many different places and stages in life. It's a good journey, and even the low spots can hold lessons, both for us and others with whom we may share this pilgrimage. As I enter my fifth decade in life, with most of those years spent in His service, I am more excited about life and ministry today than ever before. Don't settle for a "less than" life, when God has called you to uniquely impact this world for His glory. Enjoy where you are now, with the places and faces that are a part of this season, and know that good things are ahead, down the road and around the corner, in the next season of your life.

SO GREAT A PRICE

...knowing that you were not redeemed with corruptible things, like silver or gold, from your aimless conduct received by tradition from your fathers, but with the precious blood of Christ, as of a lamb without blemish and without spot. (1 Peter 1:18-19)

What is a person worth? How does one gage one's own value? For too many people, their sense of value is determined in all the wrong ways; by parents who told them they were an unwanted accident, by school mates that bullied or belittled them, or perhaps even worse, by being ignored and overlooked. It is unquestionably true that what we aspire to in life, and indeed, what we accomplish, is very much connected to our sense of value and self-worth.

Those who are affirmed by their parents and peers, usually go into life with a greater sense of confidence, believing they can do whatever they set their minds to. They fully expect to succeed because they have been led to believe they were made for nothing less. On the other hand, those who have been minimized and marginalized by others their whole life often feel that any but the smallest dreams and aspirations are beyond their reach. If they can just get by unnoticed, fly beneath the radar, then that might be best, since most of the attention they have received in life has tended to bring discouragement and pain. No matter how unfounded such beliefs might be, their perception become their reality until something happens to open their eyes to their true value.

It has been said that beauty is in the eye of the beholder, meaning that one man's trash may indeed be another man's treasure. For example, I love leather. No, I mean it. I REALLY love leather. In fact, in my opinion, birthdays and Christmas are just opportunities for me to get another nice leather brief or bag of some kind. I have a few nice pieces I've collected over the years that I use for toting my Bible, notebooks, computer, and other items. I trade using one bag for another from time to time. For sure, if you were to see most of these, especially if you are not "into" leather, you would find it hard to believe the price that I, and those who've purchased them for me as gifts, have paid for some of them. I don't have a lot of valuable things, really, but when it comes to leather, I love the best!

If you were to see these bags when I bring them out of the closet, or the garage where some are stored now, they probably wouldn't look too impressive to you. Without anything in them, they lose their shape and look like just so much crumpled leather, and in some cases, even pretty *worn* pieces of crumpled leather. But to the trained eye, or the one who knows who made these bags, they are very valuable. I tried buying just such a bag once on eBay for a couple hundred dollars, hoping others would not recognize the piece for what it was. My bid didn't even come close, as the bag eventually sold for several hundreds of dollars more than I had to spend on it.

The problem with a lot of people is that they fail to see real quality when it's in front of them. If that's true of leather, how much more is it true of people! Who could have seen the brilliance of Helen Keller or the potential in a young Albert Einstein before they blossomed into the people they ultimately became? Both were thought to be hopeless by societal standards before time revealed them to be people who would change the world. History is full of people who were discarded as worthless until someone looked beyond the surface and discovered that they were priceless.

When it comes to *your* value, you first must realize that regardless of what you look like to others, your value is in *Who* made you. Yes, you ARE all that! At least, you are to God. When it came to the price He was willing to pay to restore you to fellowship with Himself, no currency in this world could pay the price, so He paid with the blood of His only begotten Son. It sounds trite, and it has been said many times, but it is nonetheless true: if you had been the only person who needed saving, Jesus would have died for you alone. No greater statement could be made as to how highly God values you than to say you were *worth* the blood of Jesus. For countless generations the redeemed have sung about the precious blood of Jesus. It is without a doubt the most precious commodity in the universe, and yet it was that very blood that God gave to secure your redemption.

Every person has inherent value. That is obvious by the fact that God would pay such a price to redeem us. We were each made in the image of God to have fellowship and relationship with the Almighty. But there is a difference in *inherent* value and *realized* value. Those bags I own have a certain inherent value, but that value may not be as obvious to everyone. In fact, it may be appreciated by only a select few. For most people, the value of those bags is *realized* as they serve the purpose for which they were made (which is not collecting dust in my garage). God does not want you living a "less than" life! He wants you to know not only your *inherent* worth to Him. He wants you to *realize* the value you have in the life He's called you to live.

Mark Twain famously said, "The two most important days in your life are the day you were born and the day you find out why." What enabled us to see the value of certain people, such as Einstein, the Founding Fathers, Abraham Lincoln, or any other famous historical person, is that they discovered the purpose for which they were born and served that purpose with their whole heart. Nothing could increase your inherent value to God. That was established by the price he set on you when He redeemed you with the precious blood of Jesus. But what will cause your value to have *expression* is discovering and serving God's purpose for your life. You were designed by God for a life of significance (see Ephesians 2:10), and your highest contribution will be made when you let others see that you are not empty, but filled with God's grace and ability (see Ephesians 4:7 and 1 Peter 4:10-11); not shapeless, but designed by the Master Craftsman to both carry and communicate His life and love to those whose value is yet to be realized.

JOURNEY TO A STRONG FINISH

Not that I have already attained, or am already perfected; but I press on, that I may lay hold of that for which Christ Jesus has also laid hold of me. Brethren, I do not count myself to have apprehended; but one thing I do, forgetting those things which are behind and reaching forward to those things which are ahead, I press toward the goal for the prize of the upward call of God in Christ Jesus. (Philippians 3:12-14)

Nobody really remembers a good start, but everyone remembers a strong finish. I've never heard any announcer of an Olympic event say, "Well, he finished dead last, but he sure looked good coming out of the blocks!" There are no trophies or rewards for starting well. In fact, having to overcome a weak start to win in the end can make the victory all the more glorious and dramatic.

Throughout history, and in the scriptures, we have lots of examples of individuals who overcame a dismal beginning in life only to end up having made a great contribution to mankind and the Kingdom of God. Others have failed somewhere in the middle of their race, but recovered from the discouragement of having blown a good start and finished strong.

"For a righteous man falls seven times and rises again" (Proverbs 24:16). Satan desires to rob you of your hope. Hope is that sure and certain expectation that good will come. The devil will try to paint every failure as the curtain closing on your chance to live a significant life for God. When we have a setback or any kind of failure in life, we must realize that God has already provided mercy and grace to assist us in recovering from our losses (see Hebrews 4:15-16). While we don't want to minimize the importance of personal accountability and repentance, we must learn to recover from our setbacks quickly. Stewing over past sin, failure, or loss is to set up shop in the devil's house of lies and live defeated, when all the time Christ has purchased your victory and made a fresh start available by His grace.

Included among those whose feet slipped from the path on their way to serving God's purpose for their life, is a list of the Bible's best and brightest. Abraham, Moses, Samson, David, and Peter are just a few who went on to do great and memorable things after having recovered from personal sin and failure. The Bible does not shield us from the dark side of our heroes' lives, but lets us know that just as they survived failure to go on and do great exploits, so can we. They did not achieve what they did because *they* were great, but because God was gracious and merciful and saw in each of them an instrument He could mold to His purpose. Often, God's dealings with these men required a lifetime before they became the men that we ultimately see in scripture. Jacob, for example, whose name means "supplanter" or "deceiver," is finally renamed Israel, or "Prince with God," after a final wrestling with God that left him literally changed for the rest of his days. Like so many in the scriptures, he grew into the man God called Him to be after a life of progressive change, with God ever present in the shadows, moving him toward his destiny and true character.

The same is true with each of us. God has a great plan for your life, and He intends for you to fulfill it, even if the devil has tried to convince you that you have lost your best opportunity to do your part for the Kingdom. It helps to remember that since God is omniscient and knows all things, including our future, He is never caught by surprise, nor is He ever disappointed. He saw both the mountaintops and valleys of our life, and He has a plan to help us successfully navigate both and come out as victors through Jesus Christ. As with Jacob, there will be some lessons to learn along the way.

Jeremiah 29:11 is an often quoted verse: "For I know the thoughts that I think toward you, says the Lord, thoughts of peace and not of evil, to give you a future and a hope." As positive as this sounds, someone has rightly said that it is a good verse in a bad chapter in an even worse book, meaning that the children of Israel were going into bondage because of their continued rebellion and idolatry. Despite their failure, God's calling upon the nation remained intact, even though they were going to have to endure captivity for a season due to their poor choices. As the prophet later says of God's unfailing mercies:

Through the Lord's mercies we are not consumed,
Because His compassions fail not.
They are new every morning;
Great is Your faithfulness. (Lamentations 3:22-23)

The longsuffering and mercy God showed His servants in the Old Testament is not lessened toward his children in the New Testament. As the writer to the Hebrews says, "For we do not have a High Priest who cannot sympathize with our weaknesses, but was in all points tempted as we are, yet without sin. Let us therefore come boldly to the throne of grace, that we may obtain mercy and find grace to help in time of need" (Hebrews 4:15-16). Likewise, Paul tells us, "For the gifts and the calling of God are irrevocable" (Romans 11:29). Your background does not have to determine your foreground, and your past failures do not define you. As the children of Israel discovered, while God always forgives us when we humble ourselves before Him, that does not mean we will recover all the ground we lost overnight.

Recovery from failure or setback is usually not an event but rather a process. This means that you will not always pick back up in exactly the same spot where life's challenge derailed you. Very often, there will be a journey of growth and discovery that will be transformative. This "scenic route" back into God's will and purpose for your life is not time in the penalty box, but rather an opportunity for personal growth and change. Along this path to His purpose, God will use you, perhaps in ways you never thought possible, and teach you lessons that you may have never learned otherwise. One of the greatest pieces of advice for anyone who finds themselves on such a path is to realize that God *is* working His plan out in your life, even in those moments when you feel you have been placed on Heaven's back burner. The best thing you can do is *not resist* the process, even when you would swear that God has completely forgotten about you. He hasn't, but there is a work that must be completed, and sometimes it takes time. He is not just interested in what you will *do* for Him, but in whom you are *becoming*.

Take heart and know that wherever you are in this process, God will continue to move you into that ultimate place of purpose and usefulness to which He has called you. He is longsuffering and has already planned the route by which He will take you to transform you into that man or woman He has called you to be.

THE TRUTH BEHIND THE LIE

But God shows his anger from heaven against all sinful, wicked people who suppress the truth by their wickedness. They know the truth about God because he has made it obvious to them. For ever since the world was created, people have seen the earth and sky. Through everything God made, they can clearly see his invisible qualities—his eternal power and divine nature. So they have no excuse for not knowing God. (Romans 1:18-20 *New Living Translation*)

Why is it that some of us can look at a magnificent sunset, the starry night sky, or any other of the countless beauties of nature and say, "There has to be a God!" while others will look at the same wonders and dismiss any possibility of a transcendent Creator by saying that it is all the result of an unguided, natural process that began with the Big Bang? Why do some look into the night sky and see the Divine while others look up and see a random collection of super-heated gases and space rocks?

Don't be fooled for a moment by someone telling you that it was the scientists and their scientific evidence that led them to disbelieve in God. There are too many other scientists who look at that same evidence and interpreted it in a completely different way, seeing the clear tokens of an intelligent Designer behind the wonders of the cosmos. The fact is, there's more to what make up our beliefs than the evidence in a test tube or the empirical data of researchers.

The Bible tells us that God has left a clear witness of Himself in all that He made. As the Psalmist said, "The heavens declare the glory of God; and the firmament shows His handiwork" (Psalm 19:1). It is as though the stars, and all that God has created, cry out and bear witness to His reality. Yet there are those who profess a skepticism, and more than that, an adamant disbelief in God. I don't doubt that they mean what they say, but what I DO doubt is that they are fully aware of what is truly behind their lack of faith.

The Bible clearly says that God has given evidence of Himself. What then? How do we reconcile this with the fact that there are so many who refuse to acknowledge what many of us would call the *reality* of God? Paul, in the passage quoted at the top of this article, says that God's wrath burns against sinful people, NOT because they *misread* the evidence, but rather because they "*suppressed* the evidence by their wickedness." They weren't incapable of reading the signs, rather they didn't *want* to read the signs!

If we are honest, we know that we all bring our presuppositions to any discussion or debate, along with our biases and prejudices too. We hear it in the old, humorous statement, "My mind is made up, don't confuse me with facts!" While we laugh at this, there is a great deal of truth to it. If there weren't, it wouldn't be a cliché! All this is to say that we believe what we believe, at least in part, because we *want* to believe it that way. What this entire passage in Paul's letter to the Romans is saying is that man, being a wicked, fallen being, simply wanted to live by his own dictates, pursuing his own ungodly lusts, and in order to do so with some sense of moral impunity, he simply took God out of the picture. He denied or suppressed the truth, denying his conscience the opportunity to be enlightened to its own sinful condition. After all, if there is no transcendent God to which I am accountable, then I can do what I want without worrying about those pesky consequences that come from doing something "sinful." If there is no God, then there is no objective moral law to break, and so there is, in fact, no such thing as sin! How wonderfully convenient!

According to God's Word, the denial of God's existence is not the result of the "evidence," which the Bible says clearly points to the existence of God, but in the willful interpretation of the evidence to exclude the possibility of a transcendent Creator. The efforts by atheistic scientists to produce theories to eliminate the need for a Creator can be extreme and even a little amusing at times. For example, to avoid the implications of the fine tuning of the universe to support life (an undeniable scientific fact that strongly supports Intelligent Design), leading scientists, including Stephen Hawking of Cambridge University, have posited the multi-verse theory. This little whopper of a theory proposes the idea that our universe is just one of an infinite number of universes, one of which was bound to have just the right conditions to support life. Wow, lucky us. That's going a long way to avoid the idea of a Creator. In fact, I would say that this theory, along with others I have heard, take more faith than our belief that God simply said, "Let there be light," and it was so.

Even better is the far-fetched theory of *panspermia*. (You've really got to remember this one, folks, because you won't hear anything that sounds this crazy coming from genuinely intelligent people in all your life!) This theory suggests that since life is entirely too complex to have emerged from the meager elements of the primordial soup, as materialists maintain, it must have been "seeded" here by some extra-terrestrial intelligence long ago. The late Nobel prize winning British molecular biologist, physicist, and neuroscientist Professor Francis Crick, along with British chemist, Leslie Orgel, proposed this theory of "directed panspermia." In other words, E.T. is our Dad. There are other iterations that have these "life seeds" coming in on meteor showers, etc. However, none of these various theories explain whom (or Whom) was responsible for creating the complex life in those seeds!

I think you see my point. If you torture the data long enough, it will tell you whatever you want to hear, and if the issue is trying to avoid moral accountability to God, it seems that men will indeed go to extreme measures. The truth is, however, that all such attempts to run from God are like lost wanderings in the woods. They only take one in circles that lead right back to the starting point. Man is a sinner in need of a Savior. God pierced through the veil of time and space to reach us in our fallen state. Through the person of Jesus, God came, revealed Himself to us, bore our guilt and shame, and through His selfless death, paid the price that would bridge the gap between a holy God and sinful man. That's it. That's the simplicity of the gospel. Simple enough for a child to believe but profound enough to have transformed human civilization for over two thousand years.

The ultimate discovery is this: Jesus is the answer, or as John said it long ago, He is "the way, the truth, and the life" (John 14:6). This discovery, however, demands a response. The good news is that this is an open book test. Say "Yes" to Jesus. After you get that one right, a lot of the other questions will answer themselves.

A PRICE, A PLACE, AND A PURPOSE

A woman of Samaria came to draw water. Jesus said to her, "Give Me a drink." For His disciples had gone away into the city to buy food. Then the woman of Samaria said to Him, "How is it that You, being a Jew, ask a drink from me, a Samaritan woman?" For Jews have no dealings with Samaritans. Jesus answered and said to her, "If you knew the gift of God, and who it is who says to you, 'Give Me a drink,' you would have asked Him, and He would have given you living water." (John 4:7-10)

To us in the twenty-first century West, there is nothing very unusual in Jesus' encounter with the woman at the well of Samaria. It differs little from an exchange we might have with someone at the water cooler at work or in the line at the grocery store. However, to a first-century audience, this encounter would have provoked no little wonder and some degree of shock. Lines of class and culture were more distinctly drawn in Jesus' day than they are in ours, and He was bypassing any number of societal taboos by engaging her, which is evident by her surprise and response to his simple request for a drink of water.

Women in general were little more than chattel in first century Palestine, and this woman, a half-breed Samaritan, would have hardly been noticed by any one of Jesus' own disciples. Understanding how the societal lines were drawn in those days helps us then to see how Jesus' interaction with her ascribed a value to this woman she would never have expected from a man in her own village, much less a Jew with whom she was unacquainted. To say it would have caught her off guard would be an understatement, and may have even aroused her suspicions.

This is where so many in the world find themselves today. If there is one thing that is universally true of people of all cultures everywhere, it is that we all seem to carry with us a sense of inadequacy. Even those who demonstrate the greatest bravado often harbor hidden insecurities about themselves. We all inherently wonder, "I am good enough?" I believe this is a residual trait carried over from our fall in the Garden of Eden and subsequent alienation from God. We know we're not what we should be. We know we don't measure up, and consequently we spend so much time looking for validation and affirmation from whatever or whoever will offer it. This need remains unmet until we find our acceptance with God in Christ. I believe God meets that need for validation and demonstrates our value in three ways:

OUR PURCHASE PRICE. As the scriptures tell us, God didn't redeem us with silver and gold, "but with the precious blood of Christ, as of a lamb without blemish and without spot," (1 Peter 1:19). If the value of a thing is determined by the price paid, then God surely demonstrated that we were priceless in His eyes when He spilled the blood of His only begotten to secure our redemption. The songs that extoll the precious blood of Christ are without number, and the sermons that particular theme has inspired are countless, and yet it was that precious blood that God willingly shed to secure our deliverance.

OUR PLACE. We all desire a place of belonging. The popular television show, *Cheers*, quipped in its title song that we all want to go "where everybody knows your name." It's true. We all seek for belonging, love, and acceptance. Denzel Washington's brilliantly directed movie, *Antwone Fisher*, tells the story of a young black man and his search for belonging. It opens with the image of Antwone, as a young boy, in a large house with a table set with every homemade delight spread out before him. Waiting with open arms is the family whose love and acceptance define for him the quintessential idea of home. A moment later Antwone awakens from sleep to realize the images were only dreams expressing that inward longing for a restored sense of belonging for which we all hunger. For those who have come home to the Father through Christ Jesus, that sense of belonging is found when we become a part of the family of God. As the scriptures tell us, "God places the lonely in families; He sets the prisoners free and gives them joy..." (Psalm 68:6 *NLT*).

HIS PURPOSE FOR OUR LIVES. Even the most secure child will grow up to feel unfulfilled and useless without a sense of purpose. Most of us ask at some point in our lives, "What am I here for?" God made us for more than heaven when we die. He has both a place and a plan for us. God has uniquely called and gifted you to live a significant life (see Ephesians 2:10). God has made you to be a world-changer and a history maker. In fact, God has called us all to share the revelation of the goodness of God with those who are still on the outside looking in, that they may likewise find their way home though Jesus Christ and enjoy the place and purpose to which God has called them.

There are many in our world, and within the circle of our influence, who still trudge out to the same dry wells each day. In fact, of the making of idols there seems to be no end, as men give their devotion to one thing after another, from pleasure to profit to play, hoping to find in any of these the contentment they seek. Yet every new venture and trendy diversion proves only to be one more broken cistern with no water to satisfy that fundamental thirst for value, belonging, and meaning. That thirst is satisfied only in Jesus, and He still sits beside the dusty wells of this world to show the weary wanderer where they can drink of that living water to the full.

AN AUDIENCE OF ONE

...for they loved the praise of men more than the praise of God. (John 12:41)

All of us must decide whom we will choose to please in life. It has been said that we all play for an audience. The difference is in whom we choose as our audience. We must ask ourselves, "For whose applause am I living?" There is great pressure coming at us from all sides to measure up, and to satisfy the expectations of the people who believe we are called to no higher purpose than to please them.

This tendency has corrupted good leadership by turning leaders into followers who gauge their actions by the temperament of the people. This is leadership by the polls, as it were. To this, Winston Churchill remarked, "I hear it said that leaders should keep their ears to the ground. All I can say is that the British nation will find it very hard to look up to the leaders who are detected in that somewhat ungainly posture." [5]

The desire to please and be accepted is a tendency with which we all have to recon. The impulse to please is closely connected to a fear of being unpopular, which is to many, unfortunately, the same as the fear of failing. True leadership, on the other hand, recognizes that the right thing is often unpopular at the time, and it does not pander to the whims and preferences of people, but addresses the need at the moment by recognizing its responsibility to a higher authority than the momentary pleasure of a given constituency.

For those of us who are believers, our audience is an audience of One. That audience is God and God alone. When we love the praise of men more than the praise that ultimately comes from God, our north star becomes uncertain and inconstant. This will never give us clear direction and fosters instead a weakness of character that is undesirable in any leader, and when we are talking about leadership by influence, every follower of Christ is a leader. Many pastors wrestle with the realization that making an unpopular decision or preaching a strong, uncompromising message, may cost them church members who hold to a shallow commitment. While this may seem to expose a fear of men over a fear of disobeying God, we must first acknowledge that these fears are not unfounded. Those in spiritual leadership often feel the pressure to cater to the changing whims of a sight and sound generation whose choice of church is more often based on who can best keep their attention than on who can best help them to grow.

While leadership must invariably understand where their people are, that is NOT to say that they are to pander to where they feel inclined to go. Leaders must both show the destination and explain how one is to get there, while at the same time leading by example. It is not for the faint of heart, and no true leader will do credit to his office that does not die a thousand deaths to the carnal impulse to simply please.

In all our lives we must choose what our guiding influence for life will be. We must decide to either choose to please men or God.

We cannot always choose both, but it is certain we can only do service to both by choosing to serve the purposes of God. Even the best ideals of men are not sufficient source material from which to draw our direction for life. We can learn from others and gain wisdom from the examples of what others have done to succeed in their life's purpose, but we must each hear personally from God to know His particular direction for our lives.

The Bible says, "The fear of man brings a snare, but whoever trusts in the Lord shall be safe" (Proverbs 29:25). I have found in my own tenure as a leader that many who seemed to have the strongest opinions in trying to shape the direction I was to take as a pastor were often those who did not even stay around long enough to finish the journey with us. Ultimately, our direction proved inconsequential to them, but the rest of us had to live with the choice we made to either follow God or the loudest voice in the room. Likewise, in your life, the only safe course is to trust to what you know God is leading you to do and to go where He is telling you to go.

I don't necessarily believe we are courageous by nature, but leadership takes great courage. In the first chapter of the book of Joshua, God tells the new leader of His people three times to be "strong and courageous," and in one of those instances He says to "be *very* strong and courageous." While we may love those around us, and want to please them, we must live and lead with blinders on, choosing only to play for the applause of the One who called us to follow Him rather than men; to follow the cloud rather than the crowd, and to live for the eternal reward of obedience rather than the short-lived praises of men.

MEDDLESOME LOVE

As many as I love, I rebuke and chasten. Therefore be zealous and repent. (Revelation 3:19)

This year when my son came home from the University of Hawaii, Manoa to spend the holidays with us, he had the chance to minister at our church. The last time he preached for me was in my absence, when my wife and I were away, so while I had heard the recording I was not there to hear him in person. This time I was front and center. While he said he was conscious of my presence, you would have never known it from his natural delivery and excellent presentation.

I was quick to tell him what a great job he had done, and when he asked me for some constructive criticism I was equally ready with my answer. Yes, I had some pointers for him. After thirty years as a communicator you learn a few things, and I shared some ideas that I believed would be a help to him. I knew he would be glad for the advice and would use it to become an even better communicator.

Giving my advice to him was easy for a couple of reasons. First, I knew he really wanted to hear it, because he genuinely wants to improve. Secondly, I knew he would know where the input was coming from: the love of a dad who wants to see his son achieve his highest potential in anything God has called him to do.

That is how God feels about us, and that is why He won't leave us alone. Throughout our lives God will have some things to say to us when we put ourselves in a position to listen. What we do with what He has to say will determine whether we improve to become the people He's called us to be or whether we continue to inhabit the already crowded space occupied by those who would rather stay where they are than make the adjustments necessary to fulfill God's highest and best for their lives.

What I had to say to my son did not involve rebuke or any severe correction; just some simple tips to help him communicate more effectively. However, in today's cultural climate, many have become so sensitive and thin-skinned that any criticism, even that which is designed to bring greater blessing to one's life, is seen to be mean-spirited and hurtful. Rather than looking to hear truth that can cause us to overcome our limitations, many today would rather make excuses for their mediocrity and limit themselves to an unfulfilled potential. We don't "do criticism" well as a people anymore. Consequently, the caliber of people we produce is less than what it was in days gone by when people understood that there were standards that others had a right to expect from us. For the believer, any aversion to correction and instruction that exposes potential weaknesses and motivates us to lift our game to God's best, is inexcusable.

And you have forgotten the exhortation which speaks to you as to sons: "My son, do not despise the chastening of the Lord, Nor be discouraged when you are rebuked by Him; For whom the Lord loves He chastens, And scourges every son whom He receives." (Hebrews 12:5-6)

Growth involves change. We cannot grow if we are unwilling to change, and we cannot change unless we are first confronted with those areas of our lives where improvement has to be made. This should be obvious since it's the same logic we would apply to the student in school, the new employee on a job, or just about any other field of endeavor where we are expected to learn and grow. Why should the Christian life be any different?

Often, the rub comes in how God brings his chastisement. It might be easier to take if the Almighty would condescend to come down on a cloud and deliver the news Himself, but more often than not, He uses other imperfect people to speak into our lives. This happens in several ways:

AT CHURCH: "All Scripture is given by inspiration of God, and is profitable for doctrine, for reproof, for correction, for instruction in righteousness, that the man of God may be complete, thoroughly equipped for every good work" (2 Timothy 3:16-17). I'll never forget the day when as a traveling minister I was sitting in a church service listening to a message my pastor was preaching. That sermon was finding every gap in my defenses. Sometimes the Word can be like the plaque rinse I saw advertised on television years ago that claimed it "got into all the hard to reach areas!" That's what the Word is supposed to do (see Hebrews 4:12-13). As the message continued to find its target in my already smarting heart, I began to wax defensive and harden my heart to the rebuke. It's easy enough for any of us to do when we're being confronted with areas of our lives we need to examine. Later, when studying the above referenced passage in Hebrews, the Lord brought that instance back to my memory and said to me, "That's what you did. You despised the chastening of the Lord!" God may use human agency, but it is He who is doing the chastening though His Word. When we harden ourselves and become unteachable it is not man that we are rejecting, but God.

THROUGH RELATIONSHIPS: Ephesians 4:15 says that by "speaking the truth in love" to one another, we "grow up into... Christ." Some people think speaking in love means never saying anything that could possibly offend, but while different friends may have varying styles of delivery, only we can choose whether we'll be offended or listen for the voice of God in what they have to say to us. Obviously, there will be those who will use any opportunity to tell us how they think we should be living our lives, but there are also those whom God has placed in our path to help us get over the sticking points in our character and behavior. If we are honest with ourselves, we know when those voices are speaking, and we must choose to "receive with meekness the implanted word, which is able to save (our) souls" (see James 1:21). None of us have arrived yet, and God will invest into us by raising up those who have a platform to speak into our lives when we are blind to, or simply refuse to see, areas where our walk with God needs improving.

IN PRAYER AND DEVOTION: God speaks to His children today. You may never hear a voice, per se, but every child of God should know that inward conviction that confronts us in those quiet times when we're giving God the floor to speak to our hearts. Sometimes it will be a verse that seems to be lifted off the page to bring light to our darkened heart, exposing areas in our lives where change needs to be made in order for us to continue in that upward call of God in Christ Jesus.

I have sat through more conversations with people and parishioners than I can number, where things were told to me that I felt needed to be addressed. On a number of those occasions I have said little. Sometimes that has been wisdom, as the individual was not ready to hear what needed to be said any more than I was that day in church when I tried to shut out the message my pastor was preaching. However, other times I have to believe I remained silent because I didn't want to put myself in a position to be misunderstood or thought critical. However, in reality this was a lack of love of my part. God rebukes us because of the great love He has for us, thus for us to fail to share truth that can spare a brother or sister from much heartache must be seen as a lack of love on our part, even if our input may be misunderstood or unappreciated.

Love does not always wear velvet gloves. Sometimes God can speak in an undeniably convincing way that sets us aback and may even sting, if that is what is needed to get our attention. Paul told Timothy to "Preach the word...Convince, rebuke, exhort, with all longsuffering and teaching" (2 Timothy 4:2). God will tailor the delivery to our need, and He may just use someone in our life who loves us enough to risk our wrath to get the message across. Again, we are the only ones who can choose to let the Word of God do its work in us or deflect those constructive opportunities to change and grow.

Remember, not everyone loves you enough to tell you the truth. The Bible warns us of that when it says, "Wounds from a sincere friend are better than many kisses from an enemy." (Proverbs 27:6 NLT). One of my favorite preachers has often said, "When someone is buttering you up, they're getting ready to take a bite!" Not every voice of flattery is meant to serve our best interests. Most of us know that confronting a friend with truth is not the most enviable task, so when we do find a faithful friend who is willing to take the chance to truly help us grow, we need to thank God for the gift He has given us. After all, only a God who doesn't care how we end up would fail to correct us when we need it.

> As you endure this divine discipline, remember that God is treating you as his own children. Who ever heard of a child who is never disciplined by its father? If God doesn't discipline you as he does all of his children, it means that you are illegitimate and are not really his children at all. (Hebrews 12:7-8 *NLT*)

ALL IN A DAY'S WORK

But, beloved, do not forget this one thing, that with the Lord one day is as a thousand years, and a thousand years as one day. (2 Peter 3:8)

We are all in such a hurry. The frenetic pace of life in our culture is simply relentless. We say it and hear it all the time: "I'm so busy!" Yet for all the rush, I'm not sure at all that we get any more done. We are busy with business; preoccupied with being preoccupied. If you were to suggest that someone should take an hour to merely sit and do nothing but think, meditate on scripture, or even pray, there's a good chance that even many Christian's would protest saying, "I can't sit around doing *nothing!* I have too much to do!" We all know that we have become victims of a culture which we have ourselves created. The problem is that while many of us are busy playing victim to a world in a rush, God is not. He is not subject to our schedules, nor is He likely to "pick up the pace of His game" so we can move on to the next thing scheduled in our smart phone calendar. He's just not in a hurry, and if we're going to hear from Him, or keep pace with His will, plan, and purpose for our life, we're going to have to learn to wait on Him.

It is my great personal ambition to live a God-made life. I want to live a life connected to His purpose, not one controlled by personal ambitions or other men's agendas. At any cost, I want to live the life He intends that I should live for His glory, the one He ordained for me from before the foundations of the world (see Ephesians 2:10). Sometimes that means waiting. Not because God is running behind, but because *we* are. There are aspects of our character still to develop, habits of faithfulness to establish, and lessons of dependency upon God yet to learn.

Moses became aware of the call upon his life somewhere around forty years of age. In his premature attempt to speed up God's destiny for His life as liberator of the Hebrews, He killed an Egyptian and became a fugitive on the backside of the desert for forty years. Only when all personal ambition was gone, and Moses had resigned himself to a quiet life as a shepherd, did God show up in a burning bush to say that the hour had at last come for him to lead the Children of Israel out of bondage. His youthful fire extinguished and his ego tempered, Moses was now fully aware that his sufficiency was entirely in God alone. Indeed, the Bible testifies that he was the humblest man on the face of the earth (see Numbers 12:3).

Abraham and Sarah also thought God needed help getting things done. The aging patriarch allowed his barren wife to convince him that he could expedite God's promise of an heir by sleeping with Hagar, Sarah's maid, who would then bear him a son. Their unbelief and impatience brought unrest to their home and ultimately resulted in the banishing of Hagar and Ishmael, whom God rejected as a man-made substitute for the true fulfillment of His word. God did ultimately fulfill His promise to Abraham, but once again, it was after

Abraham and Sarah were without the physical means of bringing it to pass on their own. It was an older but much wiser Abraham who finally held his son aloft, understanding at last that the Almighty is faithful, even if that means waiting until His work in us is complete, so that His promise might come to pass.

As the scriptures promise, "He who has begun a good work in you *will complete it* until the day of Jesus Christ" (Philippians 1:6, *emphasis mine*), but that does not mean it will be in the time frame of our choosing. In my own life, I have grown very impatient with God's process any number of times. When it seemed God was leading me into a new season of ministry, my eagerness to dive in immediately blinded me to the painstaking preparation God had made to make the endeavor succeed. Like a child at Christmas I was ready to rip the wrapping off the gift and enjoy it without appreciating what was involved in bringing it to pass in my life.

For example, after a six-year season of traveling ministry, much of which was spent in the New England states, God led me to start a church in Vermont. It was only after I sat back and saw the over-arching plan of God that I realized He had allowed me to build relationships with other churches and pastors throughout New England for six years, all the while intending that I would eventually come and build a work in the area. Those connections were instrumental in the work we built there. Had I seen the end game of God's plan early on, I'm sure I would have wanted to bypass the process and go straight to planting the church, in which case I would have lacked the considerable support I enjoyed from the churches we had gotten to know over the many years of traveling ministry. I am sure that this propensity in us to leapfrog over God's process is why He is so stingy with the details. He operates on a need-to-know basis, and much of the details He often determines we just don't need to know!

In the end, we need to realize that what seems to us a great deal of time is, in reality, just a passing moment from God's perspective. It's all in a day's work for Him. For us, time may seem to be dragging by and our life wasting away while we're stuck, marking time and going nowhere. However, it's during those times when we seem to be going nowhere, that we're really in God's cocoon of transformation, where the necessary character is being formed which will sustain us through the challenges we will face as we walk out God's purpose for our lives.

THE TEMERITY OF ANONYMITY

Therefore, my beloved, as you have always obeyed, not as in my presence only, but now much more in my absence, work out your own salvation with fear and trembling; for it is God who works in you both to will and to do for His good pleasure. (Philippians 2:12-13)

Who we are when we are alone with no one watching is the true metric that measures our progress in the Christian life. This is our unedited, nonperforming self. Regardless of what our potential may be, who we are in practice when all eyes but God's are turned away from us is who we really are at the most pragmatic level. This is the true measure of our growth and maturity as believers.

Certainly, we look much better from our positional standing in Christ, but the degree to which we have worked out our salvation in daily practice reveals the man or woman we have become so far. Paul's praise of the Philippians to be obedient to the truth in his absence, as well as in his presence, is true praise indeed. It is all too common for even the best intentioned of believers to put their best foot forward in the presence of others, only to relax their vigilance behind closed doors or away from the crowd.

Anyone who has traveled often will tell you that there is a strange thing that happens when we find ourselves alone in a place where we are known to no one. Suddenly, for many, the fences that have kept them living within proper boundaries are gone, and they are aware that they are free to express a side of themselves they would never even admit existed in the presence of friends or family. I have heard seasoned veterans of traveling ministry admit to hearing the seductive voice of temptation whisper in their ear when they were far from home and from the restraining influences of those whose presence helps to keep them accountable. In such scenarios we find out our true mettle as our faith is tested and our commitment tried.

However, there is a new form of anonymity in our society behind which many are revealing a horrible, even wicked boldness. It is the anonymity of social media. Recently, during the Super Bowl season as much discussion and "chatting" was going on regarding the prospects of different teams, I saw a post that some man directed toward a woman who happened to express her opinion about one particular team. The hateful vitriol he spewed out at this woman was undoubtedly, to my mind anyway, only something he had the temerity to do because there was little to no possibility of reprisal. I sincerely doubt that he would have said to her in person what he wrote online had it been in a room filled with other people, or in the presence of the woman's husband, who, for all he knew stands 6'5" and weighs 265 lbs. However, on social media, people who are most likely cowards in the presence of others are suddenly as bold as a lion, demonstrating a hostile disrespect toward anyone who dares to express an opinion different from their own. It would almost seem that it becomes a release for people of small moral and emotional stature to express a fearlessness they don't possess in any other arena of their lives.

Certainly, there is plenty to find on any social media platform to offend, since it is a venue where unbridled opinions are forcefully expressed with no room or tolerance for open, honest debate or discussion. However, how we respond in such times tells us more about ourselves than the people with whom we may have a disagreement. To me, it is just one more sad but undeniable piece of evidence demonstrating the disintegrating fabric of civility in our society.

Interestingly, this kind of thing is not new. The apostle Paul himself was accused of this kind of duplicity by upstart false apostles who were endeavoring to undermine his credibility to the Corinthian believers. Paul quoted and then countered their criticisms.

"For his letters," they say, "are weighty and powerful, but his bodily presence is weak, and his speech contemptible." Let such a person consider this, that what we are in word by letters when we are absent, such we will also be in deed when we are present. (2 Corinthians 10:10-11)

Paul was essentially saying, "The person I am when writing to you while absent is the same person you'll find me to be when I'm present!" Paul was not one to use the safety of distance to offer correction he would have avoided in their presence. Paul was the same wherever you found him because he had matured to a place in Christ where he didn't need to put on a false front. He was who he was in all circumstances, before all audiences, or in that time when it matters most – when there is no audience at all.

The sad fact is that what we are seeing on these social media platforms is not some new, monstrous version of people, emerging by way of the transforming effects of the Internet. The reality is that we are at last finding out what we as a society have truly become. This bold, brash, disrespectful persona is not the Mr. Hyde being expressed out of a normally calm and civil Dr. Jekyll, but rather this is the true Dr. Jekyll, honestly and finally revealed.

As believers we must learn to respond to this new kind of anonymity with the steady consistency of character that any disciple of the Lord should demonstrate when faced with any other kind of temptation. Whether we stand before a crowd or are watched by the eyes of God alone, we stand or fall in our own character, choosing to either be strengthened or cheapened in our walk with God and before the eyes of men. In the end we are who we are, and we have to live with the real version of ourselves that we alone, outside of God, truly know.

RUNNING WELL

Therefore, since we are surrounded by such a huge crowd of witnesses to the life of faith, let us strip off every weight that slows us down, especially the sin that so easily trips us up. And let us run with endurance the race God has set before us. (Hebrews 12:1 *New Living Translation*)

Many, many years ago, I became the unlikeliest of track stars. Ok, I wasn't exactly a star, but my beginnings as a sophomore on the Junior Varsity track team actually produced some surprising results. I was not a particularly gifted runner, but I ran on nerves, and when the starting gun was fired I found that my pace kept me in front of the pack all the way to the finish line. My first three races, if memory serves me correctly, all proved to be first place finishes. I had never distinguished myself in sports before, and I was elated with the success I was having. In a couple of those races I stood alone representing my school while my competition had several runners representing theirs. The success was short-lived, but I even got to race (and win) against three boys from the now famous McFarland High School track team of Disney fame. Of course, that was against different boys in a different era, but let us not quibble about the details. This is my story, after all!

However, my greatest challenge on the track was not against McFarland or any other team I raced against. In fact, the race that made me the most nervous in my single year as an 880 runner was when there was no one racing against me at all. I stood alone, the sole runner in the Junior Varsity 880 race, and was guaranteed a first place by simply going around the track twice. The rub came when the officials, seeing that I was alone and wanting to save time, decided that they would run the girls' race alongside me. After all, I would only take up the one lane and they could run their race against each other at the same time. Now, suddenly, the race that should have been the easiest of my year became the race of my life!

To give this story a little perspective, you need to understand that the last time I had been involved in any kind of athletic endeavor with these girls was when the boys' eighth grade basketball team played a practice game against the girls' eighth grade team. If you don't remember eighth grade (and why would you), it was that horrible awkward stage when the girls were taller than us boys and towered over us like amazons out of the jungle. They had crushed us then to our great humiliation, and now I stood poised to face these same girls in what could be the kill shot to my recently gotten success as an 880 winner. What if they beat me? I would be exposed as a fraud who couldn't even outrun a girl! This was serious. The fact that I had grown taller, faster, and stronger than these girls over the last couple of years never entered my mind. I was determined to win this race or die in the attempt. I remember it well; running the race with my head turned looking behind me the whole time until one of the coaches yelled to me from the middle of the field, "Just run! They're nowhere near you!" Needless to say, I probably logged one of the best times of the year running against a bunch of girls with whom I wasn't even in competition!

Yes, I won the race, but I didn't beat the girls. We were running two distinct and separate races. Years later, when I would preach on the theme of "Running the Race Set Before Us," this story would always get a good laugh from the congregation. But how true it is that we are often trying to compete against one another when none of us are even running the same race. Paul warned against our carnal propensity to try to outdo each other when he wrote, "For we dare not class ourselves or compare ourselves with those who commend themselves. But they, measuring themselves by themselves, and comparing themselves among themselves, are not wise" (2 Corinthians 10:12). Comparisons of this sort in the Christian life, or in ministry, are never healthy and can create a false perception in two ways.

For one, we may feel like we have failed to succeed when we compare the results and fruit of our life and ministry with others who seem to have a larger impact and greater influence. Equally harmful, we may harbor a false sense of success because we enjoy great respect from our peers, have large works, or have great monetary success. None of which really determine whether or not we are successful in the eyes of God.

The writer of the letter to the Hebrews said that we are to "run with endurance the race that is set before us." I am not running your race, nor are you running mine. The course we each run in our respective races is different from that of everyone else who has ever run their race for God. Besides this, none of us started the race we're running. We were all preceded by those who have finished their race and passed the baton of responsibility to those of us who are to make our contribution and be a voice to our generation. After we have run our leg of the race, other runners will come and add to the ground we took to advance the purposes of God still further.

The good news is that we all have the opportunity to stand in the winners' circle together when the day is done and the race is over. All we have to do is to keep to the path and run with a steady pace, following the prescribed course God has mapped out for us. Regardless of the race others are running, we should never allow envy or an unhealthy sense of competitiveness to cause us to lose our joy in running our own race or begrudge someone the success they have experienced in running theirs.

Certainly, there is nothing wrong with taking inspiration from those who have run or are running their race well, or learning lessons from our peers that keep us from unnecessarily reinventing the wheel for ourselves. But to try to do, or worse *outdo,* what someone else is doing is sheer folly. I do not have the gifts or calling to do what God has called another man to do, and unless I want to run alone, without the anointing and grace of God upon my life and ministry, I had better not attempt to do so. God has called us all to be winners, and He has given us everything we need to do what He has called us to do so that His purpose for our lives might be fulfilled.

You will begin to move toward what you keep in view. If you stare too long at what another is doing or the course they are running, you may find yourself trying to emulate their style or direction for life and ministry. Don't. You make a great original, but as a copy of someone else your potential will remain unfulfilled. Likewise, do not allow insecurity to make you feel jealous of another's success. Their success is not your failure, and if we can be big hearted enough to believe it, every success for the Kingdom of God is a success we all share.

In the Academy Awards there is a trophy given for the best actor or actress in a supporting role. They are not the primary character in the movie, but they make the story of the protagonist all the better for the role they play. When I get to heaven, I want to hear the Lord say, "Well done, good and faithful servant." I want to know that I ran my race well, but also that I was a good support for others who ran their race near mine. In the end, it will not only matter that we ran our race to completion, but it will matter *how* we ran it as well.

WHAT IT MEANS
TO WIN THE WORLD

Now it came to pass, when the time had come for Him to be received up, that He steadfastly set His face to go to Jerusalem, and sent messengers before His face. And as they went, they entered a village of the Samaritans, to prepare for Him. But they did not receive Him, because His face was set for the journey to Jerusalem. And when His disciples James and John saw this, they said, "Lord, do You want us to command fire to come down from heaven and consume them, just as Elijah did?"

But He turned and rebuked them, and said, "You do not know what manner of spirit you are of. For the Son of Man did not come to destroy men's lives but to save them." And they went to another village." (Luke 9:51-56)

There are a lot of Christians ready to do battle with the world for Jesus. The problem is Jesus is not at war with the world. I think a lot of believers confuse the world with *worldliness*. Certainly, we are to be on guard against this world's *system,* which is controlled by "the prince of the power of the air" (see Ephesians 2:1-3), and avoid conforming to this world's *values* which are contrary to the righteousness of God (see Romans 12:1-2). But when the scripture tells us, "Do not love the world or the things in the world" (1John 2:15), it is not telling us not to love the *people* in the world. It was this lost world for whom Christ died. Rather, the exhortations in scripture to shun worldliness are meant to direct us toward a sanctified, holy life, free from the contaminations of this age.

God is all about people. You absolutely cannot profess to love God and not love people. Whether you like it or not, the moment you got saved, God called you into the *people business*. This is something I have seen so many believers struggle with over the years. It's easy to love God, but people are another thing, especially if they don't share your values, your faith, or your respect for God. We might grow tired of seeing this world, in all its insolence, deny the God who loves them and has gone to such great lengths to redeem them. We might inwardly boil to see political pundits, or popular figures from the world of academia, express humanistic viewpoints that fly in the face of all we believe about biblical truth. No doubt, there is a war of cosmic proportions going on for the soul of our nation (indeed, our world) as we speak.

In the light of all this, it is easy to see how some of us in the Church could wax a bit defensive on the Lord's behalf, like James and John did, and wonder if a little bit of heavenly "fireworks" might not be just the thing to teach the ungodly a lesson. It sounds good, even maybe like righteous indignation. But Jesus said it is the wrong spirit, and all such attitudes of anger and resentment toward unbelievers are founded on a misunderstanding of God's heart toward them. Jesus said it succinctly when He said, "For the Son of Man did not come to destroy men's lives but to save them."

While most of us probably recognize that calling fire down from heaven is not the right tact in approaching the world, there are still often traces of this animosity toward the lost in the way we approach them, even in our witness for Christ. A favorite verse often quoted by a frustrated believer when encountering stubborn resistance to the Gospel is Luke 9:5, where Jesus said to His disciples, "And whoever will not receive you, when you go out of that city, shake off the very dust from your feet as a testimony against them." Parallel accounts in Matthew and Mark carry the same idea, but this is not a statement endorsing a desire for divine retribution to be carried out against those who refuse to believe! In fact, that is the very thing Jesus rebuked James and John for when He told them, "You do not know what manner of spirit you are of" (Luke 9:55).

In Luke 19:10, Jesus said, "for the Son of Man has come to seek and to save that which was lost." Jesus is after the lost. His desire is that they all might hear the good news and be saved. As Peter wrote, "The Lord is…longsuffering toward us, not willing that any should perish but that all should come to repentance" (2 Peter 3:9). The same love that is in God's heart for the lost has been deposited in the heart of every born again believer (see Romans 5:5). Paul was so developed in that love that he said he would be willing to be personally accursed from Christ if it could save those of his own Jewish nation that did not believe (see Romans 9:1-3).

That love is *primary* in any witness for Christ. We are not to share the good news as though we are merely discharging our responsibility to *do* the Great Commission (Matthew 28:19-20). We are not merely to witness, but to *be* a witness. Our testimony is made effective, not merely by the words we say, but by the heart out of which they are said. Proverbs 11:30 says, "The fruit of the righteous is a tree of life, *and he who wins souls is wise.*" I think that is the right word to use. We are to *win*, or we could say, *win over* the lost. That takes more than a gruff, aggressive presentation of the Gospel for the lost to take or leave. To win someone takes time, development of trust, demonstration of real Christian character, and above all, love.

If you're a Christian, chances are someone made the personal journey in their own walk with God that was necessary to become an effective witness on Christ's behalf for you. We are all called to make disciples. This goes beyond what we say or share and involves being a model of Christian character to guide those we win as they begin their own journey with the Master.

FACETS OF HIS GRACE

For as we have many members in one body, but all the members do not have the same function, so we, being many, are one body in Christ, and individually members of one another. Having then gifts differing according to the grace that is given to us, let us use them: if prophecy, let us prophesy in proportion to our faith; or ministry, let us use it in our ministering; he who teaches, in teaching; he who exhorts, in exhortation; he who gives, with liberality; he who leads, with diligence; he who shows mercy, with cheerfulness. (Romans 12:4-8)

There are a lot of things I'm not very good at. In fact, I'm downright terrible at some things. There are also plenty of things for which I have no interest and about which I don't really care that I have no aptitude. But sometimes, to be perfectly honest, I am pretty conscious, even embarrassed, about my shortcomings.

For example, I am not very handy. There are those guys who have all the tools and can fix pretty much anything. Yeah, I'm not that guy. There have been a few times, like when I managed to fix the thermostat in the condo we rent out, that I felt like one of those guys for a fleeting moment. But in reality if it's not obvious, or if it's going to take more than a Phillips head screw driver, I have to call my wife. My Dad used to love to tell everyone about the time he was going to teach me how to work on cars. I had my head stuck under the hood, or so he says, and when he turned to explain something to me, I was gone. I don't really even remember the occasion at all, and would prefer to believe that I had some pressing business that demanded my attention elsewhere, even if I was only ten or twelve at the time.

Another area where I have no skill is in wrapping presents. I am not sure who invented wrapping paper, but I imagine them thinking of me and laughing and laughing and laughing as they were coming up with the concept. Wrapping is more stressful for me than undergoing dental work. In fact, I am the person for whom gift bags were made. Stick it in, add a little tissue paper, tape it shut. Done. No muss, no fuss! Wrapping is pure evil, and when Christmas comes along, the cute little images of reindeer and elves on the paper become wicked little beasts mocking my futile attempt to produce something remotely resembling anything that will inspire happiness and joy in my loved one's lives. Even my wife likes to sit across from me while I wrap, just to watch. It's one of those occasions in which disbelief and amusement coalesce together in her expression as she watches, often shaking her head and looking at me with something like pity in her eyes.

I expose these shortcomings because this is a side of my life that not everyone sees. I am a leader, and as a pastor, most people see me serving in my "sweet spot," either preaching and teaching the Word of God or casting vision for what God has spoken to us as a church to accomplish for the Kingdom. I am in my element there, and I am conscious in those moments of an ability given me from God to impart supernaturally to His people. I love what I do, and I spend a great deal of time endeavoring to improve and get even better in fulfilling of God's call upon my life.

Yet even in the church I am very conscious of areas where I am not at my best. There are certain areas necessary to the efficient running of a church for which I am not particularly gifted. While I love casting vision and talking about the broad strokes of the plan of God, I am very dependent upon people gifted in organization and detail to help get us there. I understand the need for well run children programs, but while I know what we need in general, I don't seem to be particularly gifted in that area either. My wife, on the other hand, has been teaching the first grade for nearly thirty years, and I am convinced she has the power to hypnotize children and bend their will to her bidding! I marvel at others in our church, mature beyond their young years, who are so selfless in their service on behalf of children who are not their own.

Others in our church are great servers and simply get things done that need doing without much fanfare or drama. We come to church to find that it is clean, and everything is in its place, ready for service. Some in the church, crafty with wood and such, have added to its decoration and have vision for other improvements yet to come. Now, when I look at our church, I see a wide range of talents, which have been expressed in everything from the tidiness of the sanctuary to the refrigerator full of snacks for the Sunday School kids.

Fortunately for me, I don't have to be good at everything, and no one seems to expect me (or want me) to try. In fact, that is my point. I think we too often focus on the things we are not particularly good at, seeing these as shortcomings that need to be addressed, rather than realizing that in our inabilities we have simply identified an area of need for which others are obviously gifted. While we want to work on our weaknesses where character is concerned, in the area of giftedness I think it is far more important that we simply soar with our strengths. To use Paul's analogy of the body, not everyone needs to be an eye to be a part of the body. As important as it is to see, it takes feet to take us where our vision leads us.

We need all the members functioning in the church, doing their part, running with their strengths, and investing their gifts to make the whole thing work. Granted, there are some areas in which we can all lend a hand. But when it comes to special areas of service, God has set the members in the body in such a way that each of us express a different aspect of the multifaceted grace of God when we serve with the gifts He has given us (see 1 Peter 4:10-11).

Honestly, knowing that God has gifted me to do what He has called me to do is very humbling. I know that for whatever reason He has entrusted me with a stewardship of His ability to help build His people and His Church. In reality, He has done that with each and every one of us, by investing into our lives the various gifts and talents we have, that through our distinct contribution His purpose is fulfilled in the earth.

FIVE STEPS IN THE DARK

Brethren, if a man is overtaken in any trespass, you who are spiritual restore such a one in a spirit of gentleness, considering yourself lest you also be tempted. Bear one another's burdens, and so fulfill the law of Christ. For if anyone thinks himself to be something, when he is nothing, he deceives himself. (Galatians 6:1-3)

The scriptures say, "we all stumble in many things" (James 3:2). It has been my observation that when it comes to our own failings or the shortcomings of those we love, we are longsuffering to a fault and often quick to provide justifications as to why we might have lived short of the Christian ideal. However, when it comes to the failings of others, we are often not so generous. The late Edwin Louis Cole once said it well in one of his pithy yet profound statements: "We judge others by their actions, but we judge ourselves by our intentions."

Recently, the story broke of another high profile minister who had a moral failure. These stories are not new, but with the advent of the internet and social media, we are seldom spared the details of stories that would have been better kept out of the public eye. It isn't that people do not have a right to expect those in ministry to live up to the ideals they espouse, but we only have to ask ourselves how we would like our own failures posted online for all the world to see, to realize that this can be a very difficult reality for any individual or family to survive.

I realize that people can be pretty bitter in their hurt and disappointment, and that public figures have become fair game as front-page tabloid fodder, but we in the Church have an obligation to love and to restore those among our ranks who have taken a misstep in their life. Certainly, we have a right to expect integrity from our leaders, but what do we do when someone comes up short, when they don't meet the expectations their office demands? What about everyday believers who are not well known? How do we handle their failings?

As a pastor and a believer, I have been on all sides of this issue. I have prayed with those who have taken a wrong turn in their lives, and I have received support and prayer when my own actions did not measure up to the biblical standard God expects of His leaders. I have seen many a person gloriously encouraged as God's grace and mercy washed their sin and guilt away and restored their wounded conscience. Over the years I have had people confide things to me that no one would want known publicly. I've seen them relieved to hear that their struggles were not unique to them and realize that they were not some kind of pariah to be shunned by the rest of the church family.

We need to realize that when it comes to leaders, it is simply good battlefield tactics for the devil to try to take them down. They are high value targets, because by taking out one person, many are made to stumble. On the night of His betrayal, Jesus told the disciples, "All of you will be made to stumble because of Me this night, for it is written: 'I will strike the Shepherd, and the sheep of the flock will be scattered'" (Matthew 26:31). What he said truly came to pass, as at the time of his arrest "all the disciples forsook him and fled" (Matthew 26:56). It is simply a principle that applies both naturally and spiritually. When a leader is lost it creates confusion and distress among the sheep.

Leaders have influence, and so a leader's actions carry greater repercussions. When they fail, others are often affected adversely, and some may choose to leave the church or even abandon their faith. Some of this is because we have set leaders on too high a pedestal and attached our faith to them rather than to Jesus, our true Shepherd and Leader.

Years ago I was speaking to a minister about this very issue, and he shared a great analogy with me. He said that any of us might wake up in the middle of the night to head to the kitchen or the bathroom, forgetting that our wife has rearranged the furniture. As a result, we might trip over the sofa, step on the cat's tail, sending it shrieking through the house, and land with a crash on the coffee table. That story will become a party tale for years to come as people laugh with you (or at you) for your five steps in the dark, which landed you on top of a pile of broken furniture. Yet, interestingly enough, we quickly forget that earlier that day we took thousands of steps that were uneventful and took us, time and again, to our desired destinations.

I guess the moral of the story is that life does not end because we had a failure, and we should not let those five steps in the dark define us for the rest of our lives. Those who have had a crash deserve our love, forgiveness, support, and certainly our prayers. As one person said, "Don't take a photo of your life at the point of failure. Keep the video running. The story isn't over!" God does not keep images of our low spots, and we shouldn't keep a scrapbook of the failings of others either.

BIGGER

Oh, magnify the Lord with me,
And let us exalt His name together. (Psalm 34:3)

If you were to ask most people how they would describe the task of trying to keep everything in their lives together, make ends meet, or find time for all their various responsibilities, you might hear them use words like, "overwhelmed" or "stressed." Were you to ask them how they feel about problems in our world, such as disease, famine, violence, and war, you might hear them describe themselves as "frightened" or even "powerless," as though the reality of such modern day challenges are too enormous, too big, for them to even comprehend a solution.

Such responses would not seem unreasonable to most of us. In fact, many do not even want to engage in discussions about the issues we face in our times because we don't really believe that we can do anything about them. It's just too big. It's just beyond us. Others would admit the need for answers but might argue that they have their hands full just managing their own affairs, let alone trying to work out issues of such magnitude.

There is no doubt that our world faces big problems. Our newspapers are filled with headlines that exacerbate the hopelessness many feel, as there seems to be no end to man's capacity for cruelty toward his fellow man. Certainly, there are good things that happen, and when they are reported the positive reactions almost seem disproportionate to the tale of good deeds, so desperate are we to discover and promote anything positive in our world. What is even more frightening to many is the realization that this is not some new, sudden downward trend in man's behavior. Rather, we simply have more and better tools of communication to get the stories fed to us more quickly.

Yes, our world is in trouble, but there is good news in the midst of it all. Our God is bigger. That's not some glib Christian cliché to be invoked like some imaginary eraser that pretends to make all the world's problems disappear. Rather, it is a realization, and what is more, an admission, that we who created these problems in the first place, are not the final solution to them. There is One who is not subject to the brokenness of this world, and yet He is touched by the pain of our brokenness and has already provided a solution to the desperation we feel.

Our focus on the world's troubling issues makes them loom large, casting a long shadow on the backdrop of our lives. People plan for a future, wondering if there is any future to which they can really look forward. They plan a family, wondering if this is the kind of world into which they should be bringing innocent children. However, fear is the tool of the devil, designed to magnify only what He wants us to see. It paints a false image, robbing us of the initiative and courage we need to put our hand to the plow and be a part of a better world.

The fact is that biblical history is littered with the stories of man's desperate condition. This is nothing new to the world; it's just new to us. As one person said quite truthfully, "New news is just old news happening to new people!" In reality, it was always in the midst of dark times, not unlike those we face today, that God broke forth with those whom He would call, appoint, and anoint to bring light into the darkness and rekindle the hopes of men. From an enslaved people he brought forth a Moses to usher in a new age of freedom for His people. When the law was lost and God's people had wandered away, He raised up a Josiah to reopen the temple and restore the people back to their God. When the city lay in ruins and her people were captives in a strange land, He raised up a Nehemiah to rebuild the city and a Zerubbabel to rebuild the temple. When He needed to prepare an oppressed and downtrodden people for His coming He raised up a John the Baptist, and when man needed a Savior, He gave us Jesus.

In every one of these situations it would have been very, very easy for those whom God used to see the circumstances as impossible, and Moses was not the only one of His servants who tried to wriggle out of the task to which they were called. Apart from Jesus, none of these men were extraordinary in themselves. They were not supermen, but rather they were normal men with a super God, a God who was bigger than any challenges they faced. For the stubborn Pharaoh God had plagues that demonstrated His power. For the beleaguered exiles in the wilderness He brought forth water from the rock and manna from the skies. For the giant who intimidated the armies of Israel He had a shepherd boy with a sling and a stone, and to restore the lost hope of mankind, He gave us a baby in a manger.

Always from such humble circumstances God wrought a powerful deliverance that gave new meaning to the word "epic" and defied all odds of success. This is how God works, not through the armies of kings but with the shepherd's rod of an exiled Egyptian prince, such as Moses, who brought a superpower to its knees through the finger of God. He does not employ the four hundred false prophets of Baal who shout and spill their blood in religious pretense, but the lone, strange, and solitary figure of Elijah, who calls fire down from heaven and brings a nation back to their God. It is God and his faithful few against everyone else, and God always wins. Always.

The fact of the matter is, yes, you can have a significant, joyful, and hopeful life in these times. Yes, you can be a part of the answer. Yes, you can be confident that you are not outmanned, outgunned, or out of your depth. Why? Not because all the world's problems will dissipate and dissolve by morning, but because God is bigger. He is not frightened, surprised, or unsure of His next move. He's got this.

Once, when the enemy had surrounded the prophet Elisha, his servant, seeing the horses and chariots surrounding them, despaired of any deliverance. Elisha, however, simply prayed, "Lord, open his eyes." Then the eyes of the servant were opened to see the surrounding mountains and hills filled with the armies of the living God who were there to fight on behalf of God's man. I just want to encourage you today, and let you know that you are not alone. If you are God's child and committed to His purpose, He is with you. And the good news is, despite what you might be facing, He is bigger.

GREAT EXPECTATIONS

For whom He foreknew, He also predestined to be conformed to the image of His Son, that He might be the firstborn among many brethren. (Romans 8:29)

W e've all heard stories of over-bearing parents whose unrealistic expectations for their children created great stress on both child and the parent-child relationship. It is all too true that parents often want to realize through their children the life they failed to create for themselves. What is tragic in this is that not only are they failing to take into consideration the dreams and aspirations their children may have for themselves, but they are also trying to make of them something they are not and can never be. While our children may look like us, and share some of our genetic predispositions, they are *not* us. They are themselves, unique and separate from every other human being on the planet.

Our uniqueness is God's gift to us, and the sharing of that uniqueness is our gift to the world. It is said that 99% of our DNA is exactly like that of every other human being on the planet. It's that 1% that makes us distinct. It is from that meager 1% that our unique contribution comes. Handel's 1% gave us the Hallelujah Chorus, while Monet's gave us his impressionistic paintings that gave birth to a new art form. Michelangelo's 1% gave us the painting on the ceiling of the Sistine Chapel, while Beethoven's 1% gave us his famous Fifth Symphony. Our particular talents, gifts, humor, personality, and creativity, all come from that tiny slice of ourselves we share with no one else. It is who we are. It is who God made us to be, and to try to yield up that small part of ourselves for the sake of those who cannot appreciate our particular distinctiveness is sheer folly. We give God the greatest glory when the sound of our distinction plays its part in the symphony into which He has cast us. To do otherwise is to play a discordant note that betrays our true self and deprives the world of our singular contribution.

God is also a parent, and He too has high expectations for us. He is not reconciled to the idea of our being anything other or less than He made us, and the scriptures tell us that He will one day ask us to give an account of what He has entrusted to us (see Matthew 25:14-30). However, God is not asking us to step beyond or outside of what He has made us to be. In fact, while He has called His children to become conformed to the very image of Christ Himself, He has put within us all we need to achieve His lofty ambitions for our lives. In the salvation that comes through Christ, we do not merely receive pardon for sin, but a total rewiring of our spiritual DNA. When writing about the salvation we experience in Christ, Paul says, "not by works of righteousness which we have done, but according to His mercy He saved us, through the washing of regeneration and renewing of the Holy Spirit" (Titus 3:5).

In essence, what Paul is talking about here is the complete recreation of our spirit. In fact, the Greek word, *palingenesia*, translated "regeneration" in this verse, comes from two Greek words: *palin* "again," and *genesis* "birth," and literally means, *born again*. We are literally reborn into God's family with His life and nature that we might progressively mature into the image of Christ. Not only that, God has entrusted some aspect of His divine ability to each of us to serve Him in a unique way that glorifies Him.

> As each one has received a gift, minister it to one another, as good stewards of the manifold grace of God. If anyone speaks, let him speak as the oracles of God. If anyone ministers, let him do it as with the ability which God supplies, that in all things God may be glorified through Jesus Christ, to whom belong the glory and the dominion forever and ever. Amen. (1 Peter 4:10-11)

I have known many preachers in my years of ministry, but I have never met any two alike. Likewise, in whatever we are called and equipped by God to do, the outworking of the grace He has entrusted to each of us will take on a distinct quality that will make a unique contribution to the Kingdom of God. As with our natural distinction, we likewise have been given a spiritual 1% that enables us to make a singular mark in this world for His glory.

We have heard since grade school that no two snowflakes or fingerprints are exactly alike. In fact, the more you look, the more you see that diversity is hardwired into all of creation. Likewise, it is built into each *new* creation in Christ as well (see 2 Corinthians 5:17). God has high expectations, indeed, great expectations, for each and every one of us. He alone knows what we are capable of as we allow our unique gifts to find expression in and through our lives. One thing, however, is certain. He is not looking for any of us to be predictable, commonplace, or redundant. He has not made us to be the latest in a series, but something altogether distinct and different, that we might help to display the manifold splendor of His grace.

A STANDING PLACE

If the foundations are destroyed,

What can the righteous do? (Psalm 11:3)

I am not a builder, but I know enough about the craft to know that regardless of how pleasing the aesthetics, how spacious the rooms, or how nice the neighborhood, if the foundation is faulty, the entire house is compromised. Cracks in the walls, doors that refuse to close, or a house that is badly off the plumb line can all be traced back to a failure to get the foundation right. Ultimately, the house can fall because of something that is not readily apparent to view because it lies beneath the surface, where no one can see.

Our lives can be very much like that. Every life needs a solid foundation; something that will serve as an anchor for the soul when times are tough or to strengthen our convictions to do right when the lure of compromise seems to offer a fast track to success. Everybody's life is built on some kind of foundation. Our true convictions, our guiding principles, however, are not determined by what we *say* we believe, but by what we *do* when the pressure is applied. Jesus said this very thing in one of His parables.

"Therefore whoever hears these sayings of Mine, and DOES them, I will liken him to a wise man who built his house on the rock: and the rain descended, the floods came, and the winds blew and beat on that house; and it did not fall, for it was founded on the rock. But everyone who hears these sayings of Mine, and DOES NOT do them, will be like a foolish man who built his house on the sand: and the rain descended, the floods came, and the winds blew and beat on that house; and it fell. And great was its fall." (Matthew 7:24-27, *emphasis mine*)

Most people don't wake up one morning and say, "Today, I'm going to destroy my marriage," or "Today, I am going to compromise my convictions and engage in unethical business practices and ultimately lose everything." We may never say that, per se, but in failing to prepare ourselves by establishing certain bedrock principles in our lives, we leave ourselves open to the siren song of temptation and compromise. One thing, and one thing alone, will reveal our foundation for what it is, and that is the storm.

For the believer, that sure foundation is the Word of God. It alone is the guiding principle for our lives. While we should be men and women of conscience, it is the Word that informs our conscience and holds us accountable when the voice of our own mind begins to backpedal on what we know to be right. However, it is not enough to have a fundamental knowledge of God's Word, we must be *doers* of the Word if we are to secure a firm foundation for life.

Jesus gives the analogy of a house built on the sand as opposed to one built upon a rock. Both, however, are built where the waves and the winds would test their integrity. Of course, the house with no foundation was washed away and fell, whereas the one built upon the rock stood when tested. However, what the parable does not say, but I believe is implied, is that the house built on the sand may not have fallen all in a day. More likely, the foundation was eroded little by little, until, in the end, there was simply no foundation left to support the house.

For the most part, the big scandals we read about, whether in business or in politics, were not the result of a single compromise. Little compromises were made along the way that ultimately wore away the scruples of the person or persons involved until, finally, their house came crashing down, and as Jesus said, "great was its fall." When one fails to build one's life on the sure, immovable foundation of God's Word by being a consistent practitioner of its truth, it becomes easy to yield to the seduction of compromise; a little here and a little there. It may seem harmless enough at first, but a pattern of behavior is formed and aided by self-deception. Once such a pattern is established, the breach widens as the conscience is seared, and a sense of invincibility deludes the mind.

The truth is, we only really find out what we're made of when we're put to the test. A deep knowledge of the Bible will not safeguard us from temptation if we have not purposed to allow that knowledge to inform our actions on a daily basis. One who truly lives by the Word will soon be battle-hardened as his or her convictions are tempered in the fires of trial and test. One who passes the daily tests to stand strong may be ready for the greater challenge that comes unforeseen. The one who fails to pass such smaller tests of character, however, is foolish to think he or she will suddenly wax valiant when a greater temptation to compromise tests his or her already underdeveloped conscience. Even if we believe we're ready to face such a challenge, we must NEVER rely on our own strength and resolve. As Paul said, "Therefore let him who *thinks* he stands take heed lest he fall" (1 Corinthians 10:12). Our reliance must be on the grace and strength of God that is available to us in Christ and not ourselves.

On the night of Jesus' betrayal, He warned his disciples that they would all be offended (or made to stumble) on account of Him. He warned Peter in particular that he was in danger of being "sifted like wheat." Peter, however, vehemently protested saying, "Lord, I am ready to go with You, both to prison and to death" (Luke 22:33). Yet Jesus assured him that before morning Peter would deny three times that he even knew the Lord. As you likely know, Jesus' prediction came to pass. What He recognized that Peter did not – as many of us don't until it's too late – is that there is often a disparity between our intentions and our actions. Good intentions are fine, but if we wait for the moment of test to arrive before we prepare ourselves for it, we will be like those disciples who forsook Jesus in that dark hour to save their own skin.

Before we become too critical of the disciples for their failure on that night, we need to realize that people are still forsaking Jesus today whenever they choose the easy way over the right way, or yield to the seduction of carnal pleasures rather than following their conscience. We all need to find that standing place as believers that holds us steady in the storm and shows our house to be a house of the Master's making.

THE GOD WHO SEES

She answered God by name, praying to the God who spoke
to her,
"You're the God who sees me!"
"Yes! He saw me; and then I saw him!" (Genesis 16:13
Message Bible)

The passage above comes from the story of Hagar, the hand-maid of Sarah, Abraham's wife. A fugitive from her Master's house due to the harsh treatment of her mistress, Hagar was now alone, without any means to support herself or even survive, though she carried the firstborn son of Abraham in her womb. She had been the victim of an ill-conceived plan by Abraham and his wife to try and bring the promise of God to pass by their own means rather than trusting to God and His process. As an Egyptian, she would not likely have heard of Jehovah until she came into the house of the man of God whose wife it was that treated her harshly when she grew jealous of her pregnant servant.

This would not be the last time God's people would represent Him poorly to those who don't know Him, and there can be little doubt that Hagar did not expect to be shown mercy by her Master's

God while she suffered in her exile. Yet it was as she sat by the desert spring that the angel of the Lord appeared and let her know that she was not alone in her isolation and grief. He asked her, "…where have you come from, and where are you going?" This isn't a question God asks of anyone because He doesn't know. He asks because He realizes that we don't know. God assured Hagar that He had a plan for both her life and that of her son, and in that revelation she discovered a God who is personal, compassionate, and accessible. She came to that spring only knowing Him as her Master's God, but she left there knowing Him as her God; the God who sees.

Some years ago I was ministering in Bakersfield, California at a church pastored by a friend of mine. After I finished my message, God pointed out a young man to me in the crowd. I called him up and spoke what God had given me for him. I told him, "Young man, God says that you are his first string!" I knew I was using an analogy that referenced the sports world, referring to one who is in the starting lineup, but I did not know until the service was over what that word had meant to him. His mother caught up with me and told me, "You don't know what you said to him. Last night the football season ended. He never played a single snap. He sat on the bench all season as a third string player." Obviously, this young man was feeling all the associated emotions young people feel in the highly competitive, peer pressure driven world that is High School. But in that moment at the front of that church, God let that young man know that there are worlds of infinitely greater importance than High School football, and that while he may have been overlooked by his peers, his teammates, and his coaches, He was not overlooked by the God who sees.

In that same service there was a middle aged couple sitting in the very front row about whom the pastor made an announcement to the congregation. They were soon to be married, and everyone was jubilant on their behalf over the good news. However, at one point in the service as I was ministering to that crowd, the Lord showed me that she had deep emotional scars from past abuse. I knew God well enough to trust Him, but I wavered in doubt since they had both seemed so happy when the pastor had announced their upcoming marriage. As I began to speak in general terms about the debilitating effects of abuse and how it can cripple us in life and cause our relationships to suffer, she began to break down and weep. I hadn't even called her out for prayer, but the God who sees pointed her out to her own heart as He spoke to her in that moment of ministry. He did not want her taking the baggage of her past hurts into this new relationship, only to see it sabotaged by fear and mistrust. No one would have known by looking at her that she suffered in that way, but there is a God who sees beyond the surface and knows our every pain.

Years later I was ministering in a church in Charlottesville, Virginia, home to the University of Virginia, founded by Presidents Jefferson, Madison, and Monroe. It was in a wonderful church, and I was ministering with a fellow traveling minister in the service when the Lord spoke to me about someone in the crowd who had a problem with their kidneys. Again, for whatever reason, I hesitated and prayed for someone else before finally stepping out and describing what I had received from the Lord. When I shared the word of knowledge God had given me, a tall, young man came from the back of the auditorium to receive prayer. When we ministered to Him, God met him in a powerful way and he spent the rest of the service on his back in the front of the church as the Spirit of God ministered healing and life to his body. On Friday night, when testimonies were asked for, this young man who had looked so drawn and pale on the Tuesday night when we had prayed for him, literally bounded to the front like a gazelle. It was obvious that God had done a work in his life. He testified that he had been recently diagnosed with the same kidney condition that his mother had died from some years before. From a medical standpoint, his case could have gone the same way, but that night the God who sees visited him in the midst of a crowd of people in a local Virginian church.

These stories are not told as mere stories in themselves, but to illustrate the fact that though we may feel isolated, alone, and desperate in an indifferent world, surrounded by people often too preoccupied with their own challenges to notice us in our suffering, there is a God who sees. More than that, the Bible tells us that He entered time and space and became one of us that He might reveal the Father's love, not only in what He taught but in the most selfless act of personal sacrifice the universe will ever know. You are not alone. God sees, God knows, and God cares. He's ready to meet you right now at your point of need. If you will call on Him, you will not be disappointed. When we come to know Him as the God who sees us right where we are, then, like Hagar, we too see Him in a new way and come to know Him for ourselves.

WHAT IS YOUR NAME?

Now when Jesus looked at him, He said, "You are Simon the son of Jonah. You shall be called Cephas" (which is translated, A Stone). (John 1:42)

God knows you. Beyond that, He knows who you can be. He does not see you in the light of your limitations, but as the finished product He's called you to become. This is evident in the way Jesus dealt with His disciples. Simon He called, "Stone," or "Peter," as it is also translated. His given name was Simon, and from what we first see of him, he was anything but a rock. Simon was a man of extremes, and more like a reed than a stone, was easily blown about by the winds of circumstance. One moment he's in the Garden at Jesus' side, cutting off the ear of a man threatening harm to his Master, the next he's running for fear of capture. One moment he's swearing to go to with Jesus to prison and death, the next he's cursing as he denies he ever knew Him. That was Simon, but it was not Peter.

The Bible says that God "calls into being that which does not exist" (Romans 4:17). He did that with the stars and the planets, and He does it with people as well. Again and again, throughout the scriptures, we see God calling people to do great things who are desperate to educate God as to their lack of qualifications. Moses, a man once brimming with ambition to be used by God, had long since hung up his cape and cowl and resigned himself to be a shepherd on the backside of nowhere, when God told him that it was at last time to lead His people to freedom. He objected to being their deliverer on the basis of his lack of communications skills. Gideon was threshing wheat in a winepress to keep himself and his crop hidden from the Midianites, when the angel of the Lord found him. The angel called him a "mighty man of valor," despite all evidence to the contrary, and told him that he was God's man to deliver His people from oppression. Like Moses, Gideon tried to backpedal out of his assignment, pleading his family's insignificance as his reason for opting out of God's divine call on his life.

When Samuel the prophet came to Jesse's house to anoint one of his sons as King over Israel, David was thought so insignificant by his father that he wasn't even called in from the field where he tended the sheep. He was truly the "least" of Jesse's sons according to his own family, but God saw past the limitations of his stature and family position to the heart of a warrior yet to be revealed. In fact, the scriptures are full of such stories; men who were unlikely heroes, born to the wrong family, in the wrong town, with little or nothing to recommend them except for God's irrevocable call and His divine insight into their true character.

Like Peter, the brothers James and John were given names by Jesus as well, He called them "sons of thunder." Many have assumed it was because they were tough and reckless, forgetting that these names were not given to describe the who they were when Jesus found them, but to describe the men He saw them capable of becoming. In reality, James and John came from a well-to-do family, and when it came time for them to try to secure a position for themselves in His kingdom, they actually sent their Mother to lobby Jesus for places at His right and left hand (see Matthew 20:20-21). Essentially they were Momma's boys who tried to use their family connections to position themselves ahead of their fellow disciples. But Jesus saw past these limitations to the men they would become, eventually sacrificing much for the Kingdom of God and the Lord they loved. In fact, James would become the first of the apostles to die a martyr's death, and John would suffer cruelly on the prison Island of Patmos in his old age because of his devotion to Christ.

In fact, all these men became what God saw they could. Moses was used by God to bring the superpower of His day to its knees as he brought the children of Israel out of four hundred years of Egyptian bondage. Gideon would ultimately lead a small band of three hundred men against the innumerable Midianite army and secure a great victory for Israel. David became the warrior poet of Israel, great in battle and numerous in conquests, as the hand of the Lord brought him one victory after another. He was known as a man after God's own heart and the benchmark by which all the other kings of Israel and Judah would be compared. Simon Peter, the once inconstant disciple, became the stone Jesus envisioned Him to be. As one of the principle leaders of the early Church, he would ultimately give his life for the Lord he once denied, crucified upside down at his own request, feeling unworthy to die in the same manner as his Lord.

Regardless of the perceived limitations, whether of status or birth, whether geographical or societal, God raises up men from common circumstances to stand as giants in their generation. They accomplish great things, not by virtue of their own credentials, but by the grace of God upon their lives. So, what is your name? Like some of these we've mentioned, you might have named yourself "Stutterer" or "Fearful." You might have carried the moniker of "Insignificant" or "Overlooked." Maybe others saw you as "Dull" or "Unexceptional," but I can promise you that God has a different name for you, and that name is tied to your God-appointed destiny.

Perhaps the best illustration of this in the scriptures is the story of Jacob. Once a man who connived with his mother to deceive his father and steal the blessing of the first born from his brother, this man went through a life-long transformation. He was changed through his encounters with God and humbled by his dealings with an uncle who proved to be more than a match as a manipulator and deceiver. Before returning to visit his once aggrieved brother, Jacob had a mysterious encounter with God. He wrestled with the angel of the Lord all night long, refusing to release Him until he received a blessing from Him. Very often these encounters with the "angel of the Lord," were a *Christophany*, or an Old Testament appearance of Jesus. In response to Jacob's demand for a blessing, we read:

> So He said to him, "What is your name?"
> He said, "Jacob."
> And He said, "Your name shall no longer be called Jacob,
> but Israel; for you have struggled with God and with men,
> and have prevailed. (Genesis 32:27-28)

It was through this encounter that Jacob, whose name had meant *supplanter*, had his name changed by the Lord to Israel, which means *Prince with God*. It was not merely his name that had been changed but his character as well, and for the rest of his life, Jacob would walk with a physical reminder of that encounter with the God Who had so changed him.

God has called each and every one of us to a significant life. His purpose for you is beyond the ability of the person you are now, but He sees in you another you, full grown in His grace, courage, and ability. You'll never get there on your own, but He is with you as He was with Moses, Gideon, David, and Peter. His purpose for you is no less significant. Regardless of your deepest fear or your greatest liability, God sees a conqueror in you just waiting to be released through faith in His purpose for you.

God called a childless man the "Father of a multitude," but it started with one son born of a promise. If you will surrender to God and His purpose for you, He will make of you the person He's called you to be. Don't live by the name others would give you or that you've given yourself due to your limitations and liabilities. Don't settle for a "less than" life when God's called you to inherit a promise. Like Abraham, who bore his son at one hundred years of age, God wants you to look to the stars and believe in those things that are only possible when God has called you by name.

PLANTED

Those who are planted in the house of the Lord
Shall flourish in the courts of our God. (Psalm 92:13)

In our front yard on Franklin Street, where I grew up, we had a
huge pine tree. I'm not sure which variety of pine tree it was in
particular, but it was very tall, reaching much higher than our roof. I
grew up with that pine tree, a difficult and most inconvenient obsta-
cle when trying to play football in the front yard. Most football fields
don't have a giant tree taking up a huge part of the real estate around
the ten-yard line.

One day my Dad decided the tree had to come down. He was
sick and tired of all the pine needles everywhere, so he had the tree
cut down. I was not there when the tree actually came down. Being a
teenager, I'm sure I had other business elsewhere, but I do remember
what happened afterward.

It turns out that cutting a tree down, even a huge tree, is not
the hard part. I'm sure it took some thoughtful "engineering" on the
part of those involved, but it was down in the space of a day. What I
definitely DO remember, and was unable to escape despite my best
teenage efforts, was helping Dad "grub" the stump. Who knew there

was more tree under the ground than above it?! It took a long time getting that stump out of the ground, and though I drive by the old homestead sometimes and can't tell the tree was ever there now, it took a long while for the yard to return to any resemblance of normalcy after that stump was finally removed.

The reason strong trees can stand through the years despite the wind and the storms is because they have deep roots. Some trees look strong but are actually *sissies* compared my old pine tree. I wanted to use an oak tree as an example of strength once when writing an article, and was surprised to read that in England many of the strong looking oak trees are easily toppled in the high winds. Why? They have shallow roots. Their "above ground appearance" is really an illusion of strength; a façade easily stripped away in a stormy season.

I think this is a good analogy of some believers. All of us—every single one of us—will face storms in life. Whether we stand or topple is not determined by how tall we grow or how strong we appear, but by how deep our roots go into the soil. The Psalmist said the ones who flourish are the ones who are planted in the house of God. For roots to go down deep, you can't be uprooting a tree every few years. You have to know where the tree belongs and commit to keeping it there indefinitely. I don't really know how long that tree stood in our front yard, but judging from that stump, it must have been there when Jesus walked the shores of Galilee. All I know is that there was no storm that was going to knock that tree over.

Years ago a friend of mine lost his wife. She was tragically killed in a car accident. They had just accepted the pastorate of a church started by his brother and were beginning their life in full-time ministry together. On the trip home from their very first church service, a young man who got turned around in some road construction, struck their car, killing my friend's wife. I got a call from his brother, who is one of my best friends in all the world. His voice was so choked with emotion that I couldn't recognize the caller. When I finally understood what had happened, I made arrangements and was on a plane in the next couple of days.

At a time like that, all pretense is stripped away, and all you have is what you've really got inside you. As you can understand, my friend who had lost his wife was heartbroken, and yet as the events of the week unfolded, I saw him exhibit a strength that can only come from having deep roots in God. He was a lifer; someone who had been serving the Lord for years in the local church, in community with other believers, hearing the Word of God regularly, and drawing life from the rich soil of God's house. It showed. I saw him minister comfort to others who wrestled with all the difficult questions we ask during such times, and when the memorial service was held for his wife, at which his brother preached, many souls came to Christ.

At a time like that, many are reflecting on the brevity and uncertainty of life, and losing someone for whom so many cared can open the door of even the most stubborn heart. Yet, I'm sure that it was my friend's steadfastness and faith, so clearly evident in that time of sorrow, that demonstrated the reality of the life that is found when one has deep roots into God. Certainly, there is strength in numbers and a certain moral support that having connections in church gives one, but we're not merely talking about having other *people* in our lives. The Church of Jesus Christ is the hands and feet of Christ in the earth. It is through the Church that we participate in and experience His compassion in a practical way. It is through our church family that God challenges us to grow through relationships of accountability, with people who pray with us when we struggle and rejoice with us in every victory. In short, it is through the Church of Jesus Christ that we connect with God in a very real and tangible way.

Many try it on their own, and others go from one church to another, looking for that perfect connection that will supply that "certain something" that none of the others seemed to possess. The reality is, however, that none of the trees in my yard growing up chose the place of their own planting. Likewise, God is the Good Husbandman, who knows where you would be best planted, and by all means, you need to be planted so you can start putting down roots. We live in uncertain times, and when the storm comes, and come it will, pretense will not rescue you. A good show without real substance will not carry you through. Shallow roots will not enable you to stand. You need to be planted. Then, like my friend, you will not only stand, but even flourish in the midst of the storm.

MORE THAN MEANING
FOR THE MOMENT

...while we do not look at the things which are seen, but at
the things which are not seen. For the things which are seen
are temporary, but the things which are not seen are eternal.
(2 Corinthians 4:18)

If we are, as secular Darwinists say, "a random collocation of atoms," the mere result of matter plus chance plus time, then there can be no overarching meaning to life. We are here merely as the survivors in the age-long battle of the fittest called *natural selection*. If the materialist is right, there is no soul to speak of; just the synapses that fire away in our brains, giving us the ability to satisfy our physical appetites and survive in the hostile world of our competitors. If the atheistic worldview, which drives the secularization of our society, is right, then morality is indeed an antiquated notion and meaningless in any real sense of the word.

If the material universe is all there is, all notions of a transcendent reality, including God, eternity, and meaning, are merely the constructs of finite creatures whose ability to even imagine such things is merely the most recent development of a mindless, unguided evolutionary process. This is the bleak reality of the atheist who makes himself the sum of all things, denying the possibility of a Creator who designed His creation with intent and created man for His purposes.

There is only one problem with this worldview. It's all hogwash. In fact, it's even downright unscientific. So much so, it's almost comical when one takes even a cursory glance at the evidence with an honest and open mind. Even many naturalists today, who have not yet capitulated to the idea of an intelligent "Agent" creating the world, will admit that there is growing evidence for the "God hypothesis."

Evidence for this abounds, from the relatively recently revealed complexity of the cell, to what is known as the "fine tuning" of the universe, also known as the *Anthropic Principle*, which reveals that our universe seems to have been designed to an amazingly narrow set of parameters so as to support life on our planet. Then there is the Cambrian Explosion and the fossil record, both of which defy and create real problems for Darwin's theory of gradual mutation over time. Then there is the revelation of the information-carrying properties of the DNA molecule, which carries the genetic code that tells amino acids how to form to create the right kinds of proteins to build the body's numerous systems and structures. In short, God has His signature of design all over His creation, as the scriptures bear witness. "For since the creation of the world His invisible attributes are clearly seen, being understood by the things that are made, even His eternal power and Godhead, so that they are without excuse" (Romans 1:20).

God indeed is the transcendent, First Cause of our universe, the Author and Creator of life, and the One who knows the number of the very hairs of your head. However, knowing that there is a God and responding appropriately to that knowledge are two very different things. And, make no mistake, such knowledge demands a response, for this God is not some impersonal force or consciousness. He is a personal God with a very specific plan and purpose for mankind. More to the point, He has a purpose for your life and mine. "For we are His workmanship, created in Christ Jesus for good works, which God prepared beforehand that we should walk in them" (Ephesians 2:10).

While we live in a natural world, subject to time and space, God, who lives outside of these constraints, saw us from eternity past and called us to be a part of His eternal purpose. In fact, the Bible says that God determined the very time and place in which we would be born that we might reach out and find Him (see Acts 17:26). What the specific details of God's plan for each of us may be will vary from person to person, depending on the gifts and calling that God has given each one (see Ephesians 4:7), but there are some things common to God's call for each of us.

God wants us to know Him. Though alienated from our Creator through sin, God made a way through Christ by which we might be reconciled to Him and become a part of His family. He sent His Son to die and pay the penalty for our sins that we might know Him and find true meaning in His purpose for our lives.

God wants us to know His purpose for our life. God has invested some measure of His divine ability in each of us (see 1 Peter 4:10-11) in order that we might make our own signature contribution in the earth for His glory. It's in the pursuit and fulfillment of this purpose that our search for meaning is fulfilled.

God wants us to discover true meaning and fulfillment. So many have attached their happiness and sense of meaning to the visible, temporal things of this passing world. Relationships, a lucrative career, material success, and fame were supposed to give meaning to life, and yet the long list of suicides committed by those who were perceived to "have had it all" show that true meaning cannot come from those things attached to this temporal world. Rather, true, lasting meaning is in knowing God and in discovering and fulfilling His purpose for one's life. As Augustine said, "Almighty God, you have made us for yourself, and our hearts are restless till they find their rest in you." [6]

Jesus said, "The thief does not come except to steal, and to kill, and to destroy. I have come that they may have life, and that they may have it more abundantly" (John 10:10). This life is only found in Jesus, the Son of God. It is through Him and Him alone that you will discover true meaning and the life of significance and fulfillment that you were quite literally *made* to live. I encourage you to say "Yes" to Jesus. Say "Yes" to Him, His gift of salvation, and His purpose for your life. It will give you more than mere meaning for the moment. It will be a well of life that will never run dry.

GOD OF THE NOW

Do not remember the former things,
Nor consider the things of old.
Behold, I will do a new thing,
Now it shall spring forth;
Shall you not know it?
I will even make a road in the wilderness
And rivers in the desert. (Isaiah 43:18-19)

Tonight, after our Wednesday evening church service, my wife and I spent some time talking to one of the couples who attend our church. The wife's Grandmother was very good friends with my Mom. They were members of the same Southern Baptist Church that our family attended all my young life, and they were coffee drinking buddies as well. Many were the times I would come home to find Virginia and my mother sitting in the living room of our home, drinking coffee and enjoying good conversation.

Life among our little community of faith was pretty idyllic. I did not realize it at the time, but in retrospect, all that was needed to make the whole thing seem like a Norman Rockwell painting was the obligatory New England backdrop. Fish fries and potlucks were our social life, along with church services, school, and family vacations, usually to see the Grandparents who lived in the deep South. When one of the men in the church had to put in a new drive way, the other men came and helped pour the cement and smooth it to perfection. I don't remember contractors ever working at our church. The men got together and did what needed doing, while the wives pitched in and helped alongside.

It was a simpler time, before the days of personal computers, cell phones, iPads, or even microwave ovens. If you wanted a Chicken Pot Pie back in those days, you preheated the oven and waited for 50 minutes for your dinner to cook. I once told my son about that, and his eyes narrowed as he considered me before finally saying, "I don't believe you." It was denial. The truth is, he couldn't imagine the horror of living in such backward times. But the truth is, it was pretty wonderful. There were no school shootings, children played outside unattended and without fear of their neighbors, and the family was a Dad, a Mom, their children, and maybe the occasional Grandparent or visiting relative.

Looking through the eyes of nostalgia is like being under anesthetic. Everything seems wonderful, but in reality, like anesthetic, nostalgia eventually wears off and you remember that there were challenges then too, and not every family was a snapshot from *Father Knows Best*. It's easy to live with a filtered version of the past that makes our present times seem even more horrible and desperate than they are. Every generations looks with some measure of sadness on the new generation, as they see more and more of what made their world so wonderful vanish under the waves of progress and change. It's simply the way of things, and as wonderful as "the good ol' days" might have been, it is a mistake to assume that our best days are behind us.

I believe this is what God is telling the Israelites in this passage from Isaiah. It would be easy for them to look back at their glorious history and remember the mighty works God had done in former days, the might of their Kingdom under David and Solomon, or the magnificence of their miraculous deliverance from Egyptian bondage, and think, "I wish I had lived back in those days!" But for every generation, God has something special, and if we are focused on what is behind us, we'll miss what God has in front of us. We can lament the days when life was simpler and sip coffee till we die, or we can realize that God has an assignment for each and every one of us in the here and now. There is still a world to reach and a message of good news to proclaim to a hurting people. Our God, who lives outside the realm of space and time, never grows old or loses His edge. He is just as ready to work wonders in our day as He ever was in any generation that lived before. We can either answer the call or start window shopping for a rocking chair to sit around and reminisce our lives away.

When Elijah was discouraged, thinking his glory days were over, he ran to a cave on the backside of nowhere to have what could only be described as a pity party. No one appreciated him, the evil queen, Jezebel, had put a bounty on his head, and no one understood the pressures of being the last man standing for God amongst a nation of rebellious backsliders! There's nothing like a good pity party to make the best of us act like drama queens! God met the discouraged prophet in that cave and asked him what He may very well be asking some of us today. "What are you doing here, Elijah" (see 1 Kings

19:13)? After God reminded his servant that things really weren't all that bad (after all, the entire nation had just been brought back to God a mere forty days before), he reassigned and realigned Elijah's life by giving him a new mission. He would now mentor the next generation that would take over after his course was run.

When the day came that Elisha saw his mentor, Elijah, caught up to heaven in a fiery chariot, he grabbed the mantle of his former master and smote the waters of the Jordon crying, "Where is the God of Elijah?" The waters parted, and all who saw from afar realized that not only was there a new prophet in Israel, but that God had not gone out of business with the last generation. Indeed, God has a work that needs doing right here and right now. We are the generation on the scene that must answer the call if the same power that marked our Fathers' generation is to transform the lost world we live in today.

SHINE

For it is the God who commanded light to shine out of darkness, who has shone in our hearts to give the light of the knowledge of the glory of God in the face of Jesus Christ. But we have this treasure in earthen vessels, that the excellence of the power may be of God and not of us. (2 Corinthians 4:6-7)

God has called His people to shine in the earth. More to the point, He has called us to allow the light of Christ within us to shine. The world needs a clear, unfiltered, and unfettered witness of the glory of Christ lived out in the life of the believer. The scriptures say that the Kingdom of God is "righteousness and peace and joy in the Holy Spirit" (see Romans 14:17). Thus, the Kingdom of God is not best represented by angry people who are only known for what they are against, but by people who are living a joyful, gracious, abundant, and purposeful life of significance.

It is true that in recent times our nation has moved further away from her historical Christian heritage. Secularism is on the rise and is certainly the predominant ideology in our institutions of higher learning and in our media. We are bombarded by a thousand voices a day telling us how we are supposed to think and speak, so as to conform to the current ethos of the modern day thought police, who judge what is right and acceptable by whether it matches the prevailing cultural mood. Since right and wrong have been traded in for moral relativism, our culture today not only tolerates but celebrates what only a generation ago would have been universally condemned as profane. This is thought by some to be "progressive," but to me it calls to mind the old story of the emperor's new clothes, where group think so dominated the King's court that it took a "fool" to finally point out what everybody could clearly see but no one had the courage to admit. I think more of us need to be willing to be called foolish by those who have proposed that we leave God behind, because the truth is, the modern ideology that is driving much of our culture has no clothes!

One thing should be clear for all to see. A nation divorced from absolutes will flounder. With no North Star to hold her to a steady course, such a nation will soon be lost and discover that those who were manning her helm were but blind guides. True leadership never comes by taking the popular pulse and deciding accordingly, but by the courage of real convictions based on the recognition of what is right and true. There is a dearth of such courage in many segments of our society today, but there are those who are fighting back against these secular ideologies that are undermining our national spirit, and we, the Church, must take this opportunity to shine like never before.

Never has the opportunity for the Church been greater! If the harvest fields were ripe when Jesus admonished his disciples to "lift (their) eyes and look at the fields," then they are many times riper in our day (see John 4:35). The fact is that anyone holding on to an unbiblical worldview has espoused that which is *untrue*, and whatever is untrue will ultimately disappoint, since it does not correspond with reality. In other words, God made this universe, the world in which we live, and everything in it. He set the laws in motion that govern our reality, and just because a few men, or even a society, decide that up is down and right is wrong, doesn't mean the universe will realign itself to oblige. All false paths ultimately lead to a dead end, and we must be ready and positioned to speak to the unanswered need of the human heart when, like the prodigal son in the pig pen, the lost man comes to himself.

There is a hunger for reality in the heart of man. He may go about his search backward, and be blinded by the enemy of his soul from clearly seeing the truth (see 2 Corinthians 4:4). But the honest, searching heart will continue to search until the answer is found, and God will reach out to that man or woman to reveal Himself. Today there are many testimonies coming out of Muslim nations of men and women to whom Christ has revealed Himself through dreams and visions. God will respond to the hungry heart wherever it is found, and I have heard many a story of someone who found Christ through a simple prayer, asking God to reveal Himself to them.

What the world must NOT see, is a superficial, disingenuous witness for Christ that belies in action what it professes in word. We must be who and what we say we are. If our heart has been transformed by the love and grace of Christ, our behavior should demonstrate that transformation in every regard. In fact, if indeed we are allowing the light of Christ to shine through us, we should require little advertising of ourselves as men and women of God. Like the light of a lighthouse cutting through the fog over dark and stormy waters, our life should clearly point men to the reality of the

One who likewise rescued us. It is the quality of our Spirit-filled lives that pave the way for our Spirit-empowered witness. We earn the right to speak into the lives of men when we shine. We don't have to *make* God sound appealing. If we are exemplifying Him by the lives we live, the world will be able, through our witness, to "taste of the Lord, and see that He is good."

> Do all things without complaining and disputing, that you may become blameless and harmless, children of God without fault in the midst of a crooked and perverse generation, *among whom you shine as lights in the world*, holding fast the word of life, so that I may rejoice in the day of Christ that I have not run in vain or labored in vain. (Philippians 2:14-16, *emphasis mine*)

FORGETTING

Brethren, I do not count myself to have apprehended; but one thing I do, forgetting those things which are behind and reaching forward to those things which are ahead, I press toward the goal for the prize of the upward call of God in Christ Jesus. (Philippians 3:13-14)

God has called each and every one of us to live a significant, fulfilling, and fruitful life. Needless to say, not everyone is realizing this in their lives. Part of the reason for this may be that our moving forward into God's future plan is often dependent upon our ability to release ourselves from a less than perfect past.

The apostle Paul said that while he was still on his journey of fully living out God's highest and best for His life, he had learned to do one thing, and yet, that "one" thing had several parts. First of all, Paul had learned to forget the past. He said, "...forgetting those things which are behind." We know that God is faithful to forgive our sins and missteps in life when we own up to them and confess them (1 John 1:9). However, just because God is faithful to forgive us does not mean that we are equally faithful to forgive ourselves. Countless, no doubt, are the numbers of people who have forfeited a glorious future because they could not forget an ignominious past. Besides this, even those who have trusted in the cleansing power of Jesus' blood to remove the stain of their sin and heal their wounded conscience, are often put into remembrance of their past by others.

There is great skepticism in the world regarding man's power to change. Even the Bible asks the question, "Can the Ethiopian change his skin or the leopard its spots?" (Jeremiah 13:23), but the fact is that what is impossible with men is possible with God. I recently read a brief biography of Chuck Colson, one-time Special Counsel to President Nixon, who went to prison in relation to the infamous Watergate scandal, though he himself was not directly involved. Colson had been a tough, take-no-prisoners kind of guy who made a lot of enemies by his less than ethical way of dealing with political rivals. However, through a divinely orchestrated series of events, this tough-as-nails political operative came face to face with the power of the gospel of Jesus Christ and was amazingly transformed. His spiritual pilgrimage literally began to blossom while in his prison cell, and he would ultimately become the founder of the largest prison ministry in the world. In 1993, Chuck Colson won the Templeton Prize, a one-million-dollar award for progress in religion, which he gave to his ministry, Prison Fellowship. The far reaching effects of what Prison Fellowship has been able to accomplish cannot be recounted in any book, let alone a brief article, and even now, after his death at age eighty, Chuck Colson's life is still having a great impact on the world.

However, as I read the brief biography, which was written by a man who knew him well, I was struck by a comment the author made. He said that despite Chuck Colson's radical conversion and great contribution to the cause of Christianity and prison reform, there were still those who, even up to the time of his death, refused to believe he had changed. They still viewed him as the man once famously known as the President's "hatchet man." The same is true for many believers who miss the mark in life and fail in their Christian walk. They damage their testimony. They too often find it difficult, even within the community of believers, to find those who will see them through the eyes of grace instead of their past failures. This makes it all the more difficult for them to put their past *in the past* and move forward in the grace and forgiveness of God to the promise of a fruitful tomorrow.

I would imagine that if there was anyone qualified to speak about the power of forgetting, it was Paul. By any reckoning, the man who would one day come to be known as the greatest living apostle of the first century Church, was a terrorist in the early days of his religious career. He himself said that he "persecuted the church of God beyond measure and tried to destroy it" (Galatians 1:13). He was unmatched in his zeal to rid the world of what he considered to be an aberrant, upstart cult called "The Way." His conversion on the road to Damascus is, of course, legendary. Jesus met him in a moment of mercy that changed, not only the course of his life, but the course of human history forever. And yet, even after his dramatic conversion, there were those in the Church reluctant to receive him for fear his conversion was not genuine (see Acts 9:26). It was Barnabas, the "Son of Encouragement," who took Paul by the arm and brought him into the fellowship of believers, testifying on his behalf of the genuineness of God's redemptive work in his life.

I don't know if Paul had to face those in the Church whose mothers and fathers he had hauled away to prison. We don't have record of that in the scriptures, but I would think it likely that a man once so zealous in his efforts to destroy the Church may have had to deal with some inner conflicts regarding his former life. However, it was his faith in the finished work of Christ, and the forgiveness made available through the grace of God, that enabled him to push past his former identity in Judaism to embrace a new identity in Christ and a new assignment to build the Church he once sought to destroy. So, Paul did not stop with forgetting. He also moved forward in a new direction. He said, "…and reaching forward to those things which are ahead, I press toward the goal for the prize of the upward call of God in Christ Jesus."

We all want to reach forward to the fruitful future God has envisioned for each and every one of us, but to do so we need to learn to forget. We need to realize that while the past might be a good platform from which to learn, it makes a lousy place to live, and God won't visit you there. Don't expect God to look with you through the photo album of your past failures. It's not that God doesn't take our sins seriously. He took them so seriously He gave His only Son that we might know forgiveness, and because He did, He will not do disservice to that sacrifice by revisiting sins already forgiven. Instead, God wants us to reach for that bright promise of a new beginning that His Son made available through the cross. Besides, there are others who need a Barnabas to assure them that there is life beyond our failures and a bright hope for tomorrow.

IMMUTABLE

For I am the Lord, I do not change;
Therefore you are not consumed, O Sons of Jacob.
(Malachi 3:6)

Immutable. It's not a word we use a lot today, and many may not be familiar with its meaning, but one of the aspects of God's divine character is *immutability*. God never changes. Because of the passage of time, many things change in our world and in our lives. Things wear and deteriorate, people age and eventually die. Seasons change, and the styles of today will give way to the new fashions of tomorrow. The names that grace our entertainment magazines today will be the forgotten stars of tomorrow, and eventually even your iPhone will become obsolete, as technology will improve with time.

God, however, will forever be the same. He is timeless and will never grow old. He cannot improve because He is already perfect. He cannot learn since He is omniscient, and because He is holy, His judgment of what is right and what is wrong is eternally established by His very nature. God does not go out of style, and He cannot be irrelevant or behind the times. Because He never changes, He does not leave us. But since the dawn of time civilizations and nations that once prospered by His grace have walked away from His precepts, distancing themselves from Him to their own detriment.

Our societal values in North America are in a wild state of flux. Like the dollar leaving the gold standard, our values have left the rule of God and have degraded, plummeting like a stone. Today people seem to want the right to live as they see fit, redefining right and wrong for themselves, without suffering the consequences of being *wrong*. In fact, in today's relativistic culture, "wrong" is a *wrong* word! After all, to say one is *wrong* is to presuppose that there is a *right*, an absolute value by which right and wrong can be determined, which does not fit into the mores of a society that wants to be able to do whatever it chooses with impunity.

However, there are always consequences to decisions. If life should have taught us anything, it is that choices can cost us. America is making a choice. Make no mistake, nearly every indicator is telling us that our society is becoming more secular, leaving behind the eternal values God established in His Word to seek a new morality, predicated on nothing more solid than whatever might seem right to the individual at any given moment. The more one follows social media, popular culture, and hear people express their ideas of what is acceptable, it has become apparent that our culture has lost all sense of direction. There is no up or down, no consensus of right and wrong, and there is a great deal of intolerance toward anyone expressing a viewpoint that does not fit the politically correct, socially progressive agenda. In short, we're in a moral and ethical mess of our own making.

If there is no objective truth, no absolutes, no right or wrong, then there should be no consequence for our trading God's law for one of our own making. And yet anyone with both eyes open can see that our society is more violent, more divided, and more morally destitute than ever before. Things that used to be universally understood as wrong and evil are championed from the highest levels of society, and deemed by the masses to be laudable and praiseworthy. We think nothing of profaning the sacred and hallowing the unholy. In fact, Isaiah could have been talking about this generation when He said, "Woe to those who call evil good and good evil, who put darkness for light and light for darkness, who put bitter for sweet and sweet for bitter!" (Isaiah 5:20).

The thing about truth, however, is that it is like God. It never changes. It is immutable because it proceeds from God. Thus, what works and what does not work, is not negotiable. What is right and true does not and cannot change to conform to the whim of any man, society or nation. It is either the rock upon which a solid life can be built or the stone that will fall upon the willful and impenitent.

There will come a time when many will see that abandoning God for one's own way exacts a heavy toll. Such was the case with the prodigal, whose self-indulgent choices left him morally and financially bankrupt, but who found grace in the arms of his forgiving father. Such was the case with the Iron Bloc nations of the last century, that shut their doors to God and were plunged into seventy years of dark, communist ideology. When at last they had had enough of poverty and oppression, many opened their hearts and doors to God again and found He had not abandoned them, but stood ready to save, heal, and restore. Such was the case with Old Testament Israel that repeatedly traded their Glory for idolatry, only to suffer greatly at the hands of their own choices. Yet, God was ever merciful to the penitent, ready to send salvation to His people when they cried to Him for His saving mercies. He is still the same today.

Because He does not change, we can know where to turn for forgiveness. Because He does not change, we can know that His love is inexhaustible. Because He does not change, we can know that His mercies are renewed every morning. Because He does not change, we need never fear that His grace has moved beyond the reach of the one whose desperate hand is extended heavenward for help in the time of need.

MISSING IN ACTION

And let us consider one another in order to stir up love and good works, not forsaking the assembling of ourselves together, as is the manner of some, but exhorting one another, and so much the more as you see the Day approaching. (Hebrews 10:24-25)

In my 30 years or more of ministry, I've heard a lot of reasons as to why people don't go to church. I'm not talking about unbelievers here. I'm talking about those who have professed Christ as Lord over their lives. Often times it comes down to past hurts. Someone once accurately said that if a one-thousand-member church splits over some controversy, you don't end up with two churches of five hundred members each. Rather, you end up with two churches of maybe one hundred members and eight hundred people who will never darken the door of a church again. Justified or not, this is a big reason some no longer go to church.

Another reason people don't go to church today is that people feel they can get their spiritual needs met in some way other than the local fellowship. With the advent of the internet and satellite television, there are certainly a lot of Christian websites and channels to choose from, and if you don't like the guy on one station, you can simply turn to the next guy. Besides, you don't have to fight the crowds or even sit through the preliminaries (or the offering!).

Another factor in our day contributing to the drop in church attendance is the change in our society. It used to be a pretty advantageous thing for businessmen, public figures, or even the average layman, to go to church, even if their own personal faith was somewhat lacking. It portrayed them as having a certain moral center that spoke of honesty and integrity. It meant they were grounded and trustworthy. However, the nominal Christian is leaving the Church today as our society has adopted a more secular worldview, and identification with the Church has lost its value. Granted, most people who once went to church and have fallen away did not likely have such mercenary motives for attending church in the first place, but the end result is the same nonetheless. There is more empty space on the church pew today than there was a decade ago.

Pastors today are also dealing with a different kind of church member than they did a generation ago. Whereas people use to choose their church based on conviction, today more and more people go "shopping" for a church based on preference. It can almost be like shopping for a car, checking out different makes and models to see which one has the better amenities. Thus, the commitment to the local fellowship is more superficial, as a rule, and fewer people are willing to work out the issues they have with other members of the church family. If there's a conflict, they can simply start over at the other church down the street. In fact, we live in a generation with disposable relationships on almost every level, including marriage. If that's true of our closest personal relationships, it will certainly be true with our church connections.

The problem with all these reasons for avoiding church is that they miss the point as to why we're supposed to be going to church in the first place. The writer to the Hebrews begins his admonition to stay connected to a local family of believers by saying, "And let us consider ONE ANOTHER in order to stir (one another) up in love and good works…" (v.24). Again, to capsulate all the excuses I've heard over the years as to why people do not go to church, have dropped out of church, or simply are slack about their church attendance, it all boils down to one thing: it's about them. I've never, in all these years, heard anyone say that the reason they were avoiding the house of God was because they thought that by doing so they could better edify their brother or sister in the Lord. No, their considerations were about their own needs, wants, or feelings.

Since we live in such a clearly ego-centric society, it is not surprising that the world has this kind of influence on some in the Church, but the plain fact is that when we become like the world we lose to our ability to be an influence for Christ in the world. Make no mistake, this attitude toward church attendance is not a stand-alone issue. It is symptomatic of a much deeper spiritual problem. We may be the land of the mega-church, but while our churches have become bigger, our commitment to God has not gone deeper. All the apostles of the Lamb, save for John, died a martyr's death for the testimony of Christ, but today the sad truth is that many people can be talked out of their commitment to the Lord and His house for almost any reason. In such cases, we haven't made disciples, we've made customers, too often ready to walk away from our "product" at the slightest provocation. While this is certainly not true of many believers, it is true for far too many, and the loss of the Church's influence, particularly in the West, is evidence of that reality.

Faithfulness to the house of God is not, and never has been, a negotiable issue. Despite the hurts we may have experienced and the many other choices we may have to nourish ourselves spiritually, the Church is indispensable for our spiritual growth and health. It is there, at the local church, that one can invest into others the unique gifts and grace God has entrusted to us. It is at the local church where we develop strong relationships, which, by the way, are made, not found. It is at the local church that we learn to love and be loved by people, who, like you and me, are not perfect and can be a challenge. That is how we grow and mature. That's not to say that there won't come a time to make a change as to where we fellowship, but a good rule of thumb is to always be led out by the Spirit of God and not *driven* out by anger or resentment.

There are others in the Church that hold in their hearts what you and I need to learn and grow. Likewise, we each have things to impart to others that will contribute to their spiritual journey. We want the Church of Jesus to grow, but even more, we want it to *grow up* and reflect the full measure of the stature of Christ (see Ephesians 4:11-16). It is essential if we are to present an authentic witness for Christ in the world. Those who study this kind of thing say that only about fifteen percent of Millennials (that is those born from about 1980 to 2000) are believers. That means the fields are white unto harvest for a Church that has its focus set in the right direction, not looking only to our own needs but those of a lost and dying world that is quickly running out of time.

MORE BLESSED

I have shown you in every way, by laboring like this, that you must support the weak. And remember the words of the Lord Jesus, that He said, "It is more blessed to give than to receive." (Acts 20:35)

When it comes to the holidays in general, and Christmas in particular, it seems like they create more and more frustration every year. It seems we don't enjoy the Christmas cheer the way we used to in America. I love Christmas. Much of it, no doubt, is the nostalgic feelings that are attached to it in my heart and mind: the songs, the lights, the feelings of hearth and home, families coming together, and kindnesses shown that are all too rare at other times of the year.

It's a time of giving and receiving. Jesus had something to say about those two things. He said one was more blessed than the other. I think we have this reversed much of the time. Who doesn't like receiving? But, needless to say, the Lord of glory knows some things we don't. He said it was "more blessed to give than to receive." These words, quoted in this passage by Paul, are not found in the gospels, and thus, they were most likely preserved and passed down by the apostles and others who spent much time with the Master. I'm glad these words of His in particular were preserved, because I believe they hold the key to real fulfillment in this life.

In reality, ministry and service to God is all about giving away what God has given us. The apostle Paul tells us, "Moreover it is required in stewards that one be found faithful" (1 Corinthians 4:2). A steward is one who has been entrusted with the goods of another, and every one of us who are believers in Christ Jesus have been entrusted with some measure of God's goods to minister to others. In fact, Paul tells us elsewhere, "But to each one of us grace was given according to the measure of Christ's gift" (Ephesians 4:7). In this context, "grace" is referring to the special abilities God has entrusted to each member of His body by which we are to minister to others. We all have something to impart, and God has called us to steward well the abilities He has entrusted to us. As the apostle Peter reminded us when he said, "As each one has received a gift, minister it to one another, as good stewards of the manifold grace of God" (1 Peter 4:10).

There is nothing more fulfilling than using what God has given us to strengthen and encourage others. I have been on both the giving and receiving side of life, and what I have discovered is that it is only as we mature that we really understand the blessedness of giving. When we are young, be it naturally or spiritually, we are more interested in receiving. Certainly, on some level this is necessary, since we can only give to others what we ourselves have received. We need to be good receivers, hungry for everything God has for us, so we can learn, mature, and develop in our ability to bless others. Too often, however, we underestimate our ability to give, thinking that we have to be gifted like someone else in order to truly be a blessing, when really the key is simply to give what you have.

Recently, as I was returning home from work, I had a very unusual experience. As I was praying quietly regarding our church service that night and what I was to minister, the Lord spoke to me. The words came quite unbidden to my mind, "Shattered dreams." I had hardly a moment to ponder the words before they came again to my mind, "Shattered dreams." After those words, the Lord began to speak to me further about this. The last words that came to me were, "I will restore your dreams." That phrase was repeated to my heart three times.

I have had God speak to me any number of times regarding life and ministry, but this somehow seemed significant. I wondered if the words referred to someone I would minister to in the service that night, or if somehow they pertained to me. When I got home, I wrote the words down in my journal, and told the Lord, "You know, Lord, I may not have everything I want in life where my dreams are concerned, but I have a blessed life." I didn't really think too much more about it as I had to get ready for the service.

That night, just as I was beginning my message, a homeless man walked into our church. This is nothing new. Due to where we are located, they do so periodically, and we are always glad to have them come in out of the cold (or heat, depending on the time of year). My wife is always quick to give them a cup of coffee, even if they are just passing by outside our doors. This man quietly dozed through most of the message, not disturbing anyone, and he was still sleeping when we were about ready to lock up. One of our men spoke to him, and I offered him a cup of coffee to go. He also took a bottled water, and when I stepped outside later, he was still there. He asked me if perhaps I had a jacket he could have. I didn't have one, but my wife had a blanket in her car which she gave him.

Judging by his appearance, it seemed that his homeless status was relatively new; just a man who had fallen on hard times and was trying to negotiate his situation and, as he put it, "Stay out of trouble." Like many, he was struggling with some issues that had very likely brought him to this place in life.

Our church is very interested in helping the disadvantaged, and our people are very generous in reaching out to the needy, both locally and in other parts of the world. This has been a particular emphasis of late, and so before we even got home, my wife and I had decided to put a care package together to give to our new friend. We found an old backpack in a cupboard, put some food and a thermos of coffee in it, and I found one of my old jackets that I knew would serve him well. My only concern was whether I would be able to find him again. He had told us he was staying in an alcove between two nearby stores.

It wasn't until I was in the car heading back to find my friend that God reminded me of the words He has spoken to me earlier in the day. I believe those words were for this man. God is the restorer of our shattered dreams. Whether one lives in a Penthouse on Park Avenue or in the alcove between two stores, we all need the God who can heal our hurts, restore our broken dreams, and give us hope again. I have had the privilege of serving God in different ways over the years, but nothing I've ever done was more important than when, finding my friend wrapped in my wife's blanket, I got down on one knee and presented him with that backpack and my old jacket. I told him it had been a favorite of mine that had kept me warm once on a ministry trip to India. It was true. Somehow I wanted him to know that it wasn't just any old jacket, but a special jacket, because he was special. It really is more blessed to give than to receive.

THE GOD WHO WASTES NOTHING

Blessed be the God and Father of our Lord Jesus Christ, the Father of mercies and God of all comfort, who comforts us in all our tribulation, that we may be able to comfort those who are in any trouble, with the comfort with which we ourselves are comforted by God. (2 Corinthians 1:3-4)

You may not know this now, but your story might just be the most powerful tool there is to reach our modern culture for Christ. Today we live in what is called by many a *postmodern* society. While even the experts find it hard to define exactly what "postmodernism" is, one characteristic of the trend is that it is suspicious of any narrative that promotes only one way of seeing things. In other words, absolutes are out. Objective truth is just too restricting for the modern, or *postmodern*, man.

We live in the day of relativism, where what is right for me is whatever I deem to be right, depending on what my particular definition of right happens to be at the moment. While that almost sounds like a joke, it is closer to how many see reality than you might guess. Thus, when we try to tell someone the *truth* of the gospel, we may find that they immediately get on the defensive, resenting the suggestion that they have to see things a particular way or they are simply wrong.

For those of us who have embraced God's Word as true and authoritative, there is no dilemma here, but for those who are living according to the spirit and mindset of the age, it is a completely different matter. Today, a knowledgeable Christian who is well versed in his faith may find that his well-crafted presentation of the gospel is met with indifference, as the listener sighs and says, "Well, I'm glad that woks for you, but I'm on a journey looking for my *own* truth." Indeed, while some may be open to more familiar, traditional means of evangelism, there is a growing trend in our culture to reject any kind of dogma that aims to pin the individual to the wall with truth claims. So, how do we reach a culture that believes that truth is relative and rejects the notion that right and wrong are even definable?

There is a well-tested and proven means of reaching the seeker for Christ. That tool is your story. You can call it your testimony if you prefer, but it is the book of your life, told with conviction by one who lived it. People may reject your gospel tract, but few can resist a good story. Your testimony does not necessarily demand anything of the listener, and thus it puts them at their ease to hear the power of the gospel in story form. It tells the narrative of your life: how you were lost, how you were found, and the love and grace of the Savior Who took you at your worst and claimed you for His own. It's the love story of mercy that healed the brokenhearted and set the prisoner free.

Testimonies do not preach *at* people, but rather they draw them in through the time-tested art of storytelling. But this is storytelling at its best; not the fairytales of childhood, of imaginary people and pretend worlds. This is about real survivors who saw life's battles up close and were rescued by the One who snatched them from the heat of conflict and broke their bands asunder, even when it seemed all hope was lost. Our stories help us identify with a hurting world, who understand what it means to be rejected, afraid, bullied, or addicted. Even better, our stories reveal that there is a way out. They give hope to those still bound, isolated in the prison of their own mind, assuring them that there is One who will reach into their darkness, take them by the hand, and lead them out to freedom. Our testimony doesn't condemn anyone, because it isn't so much directed *at* the hearer, as it is simply there to tell how our life was changed by a personal encounter. They can take it or leave it, but they can't invalidate it, because it's our story, not theirs.

For some of us, there are lessons we learned in life at much too high a cost. We wouldn't suffer the losses we did, or make the poor choices we made, if we could do it again. Nevertheless, we are now on the other side of that experience, and we found a loving God who, in His redemptive grace, found a use for us in His Kingdom. Perhaps we suffered the consequences of our actions, or just simply suffered, but either way, we now have a story to tell.

You might have come through addiction, abuse, or divorce. You may have lost a loved one or failed the ones you love. You might have been ready to take your life when mercy suddenly stepped in and spared you. Perhaps, now that time is behind you, and you've worked hard to put distance between you and a difficult past, you may not want to remember where you've come from. You may even think that it is probably best you never let anyone know, but there are most likely others who need to hear the truth and wisdom you learned in your journey. They need to know that there are still possibilities for them, and they need a friend who can assure them that there's life on the other side of failure.

It's wrong to think that the only good stories are the ones where *everything* worked out for the best. Most people can't identify with those stories. Ours is a broken world, and most of us, at some time or other, have fallen victim to the harsh realities of life. That's not to say that we haven't found victory in Christ, or that we don't know the joy of salvation. We can testify that we *are* the redeemed of the Lord, and He has put a new song in our heart! However, we must be ever mindful that there are others who have not yet found a reason to sing, and it might be your willingness to reach back into your past to share some hard-earned wisdom from your story that makes the difference between life and death for that one whose hope has failed.

You don't have to live there. You don't have to identify with who you *were*. You have a new identity in Christ, and He has washed you clean and made you brand new. But He still wants you to reach back to those still lost, just as Jesus came down to where we were that He might lift us up to where He is, seated at the Father's right hand.

We have our stories to tell, and it is through them that we can connect with those still lost. Our God wastes nothing, and He will use our past pain points as potential connection points to reach those who are living in that reality right now. It might be your story that shines the light of Christ on their dark road to lead the hurting home.

THE GOSPEL'S IRRESISTIBLE LIGHT

But even if our gospel is veiled, it is veiled to those who are perishing, whose minds the god of this age has blinded, who do not believe, lest the light of the gospel of the glory of Christ, who is the image of God, should shine on them. For we do not preach ourselves, but Christ Jesus the Lord, and ourselves your bondservants for Jesus' sake. For it is the God who commanded light to shine out of darkness, who has shone in our hearts to give the light of the knowledge of the glory of God in the face of Jesus Christ. (2 Corinthians 4:3-6)

There are a lot of voices telling us to tone it down. There is great pressure to keep one's faith to oneself. It is strange that the one message we are told to turn the volume down on in our society is the one that speaks of love, self-sacrifice, grace, and redemption. If you know the story of the gospel, you know that nothing could be more heroic, noble, and necessary for the dark times in which our world finds itself.

Still, we hear from every corner these days that we can't have the gospel on display, whether on our public buildings or in our classrooms, though there seems to be tolerance for every other ideology in the public square. Christians are routinely mocked and marginalized by popular culture for their "narrow" views, while those who oppose the Word of God are free to espouse their opinions with total impunity. Who ever thought that in America we would see the day when it would be completely taboo for our nation to look to the scriptures for counsel and direction?

The greater question really is this: "Where is all this pressure coming from?" Who is it that really wants to silence the voice of the gospel in our world? Is it the scientific materialist who rejects the idea of Intelligent Design as a probable first cause for our creation? Is it the University Professor who thinks the "antiquated" views of biblical Christianity are too passé to be allowed? Is it the social progressive that wants us to shed the bonds of restricting morality so we can all live by our own relativistic values? Is it the mainstream media who know they can get a laugh by poking fun at the "ignorant" Christians who quote the Bible on their reality television shows? Who is really leading the charge to put a gag order on the gospel?

We see the symptoms of the cause in the reactions by these various groups who want to do away with the Bible's influence on our culture, but the real cause is far more insidious. There is a war going on for the souls of men. There always has been. The real enemy of men's souls promises freedom from the tyranny of the "restrictive" biblical worldview. He tells us we're free to do as we please, owing no one anything and responsible to none. He tells our young people to cast off the bonds of their parents' faith and pursue pleasure as they see fit. Yet, while he promises freedom, he himself holds men in bondage to their own appetites, luring them slowly but relentlessly toward a hopelessly dark eternity, away from the grace and love of God.

That enemy is the Devil, whom the Bible calls the "god of this world." In Ephesians he is called "the prince of the power of the air," who directs the course of men's lives, and society at large, through the pursuit of those things that titillate the senses and fulfill man's basest desires (see Ephesians 2:1-3). While he promises liberty, he himself is the ultimate slave master, holding people in bondage to their desires and lulling them into a sleepy, spiritual stupefaction.

What can penetrate the sin-darkened mind and reveal to man his fallen condition? What other story tells of a Savior, born to die that men might live? What tale tells of a sinless One who came to reveal God's righteousness, and then made a way of reconciliation between sinful man and holy God? There is only one such story, and no wonder we call it good news, for good news it is when light of its truth falls on the ears of the sin-sick man or woman groping in the darkness. Good news it is, like a prisoner hearing his sentence has been commuted by one who has the authority to pardon past wrongs. Good news it is to hear that a loving God sent a perfect Savior to lead us out of darkness and death into His marvelous light. It is the gospel of Jesus Christ, the only gospel, for there is salvation in no other, nor is there any other name by which we must be saved (see Acts 4:12).

The gospel has foiled all attempts to silence its message of hope. Its detractors have been many, but time has covered them all in the windblown sands of forgotten memory. Yet the army of the redeemed shouts on through the ages that the way of life has been opened by a selfless Savior who reigns in Heaven and brings heaven to the hearts of the humble.

This Jesus, Who died for sinners such as you and me, is alive and active in the affairs of men. He is not idle, but bends His Spirit's influence on the hearts of the lost that they might hear His voice. He speaks through His creation, which bears witness to His transcendent glory. He speaks through the messengers whom He sends to declare His truth, and He speaks through stories of rescued sinners who found their way to life at the foot of an old rugged cross. This is the gospel, and the best of it is that there is still time to embrace it. Today is the day of salvation. Now is the accepted time (see 2 Corinthians 6:2). His promise to you is that if you call upon Him you will not be shut out, for "whoever calls on the name of the Lord shall be saved."

IDENTITY

There is neither Jew nor Greek, there is neither slave nor free, there is neither male nor female; for you are all one in Christ Jesus. (Galatians 3:28)

Never is America more polarized than when we are in an election cycle. Republican or Democrat, Right or Left, Constitutionalist or Socialist, Tea Party or Progressive – the labels go on. Without question, America is a phenomenon of human government. We've gone for more than two-hundred years under the same Constitution. No other nation has come close. We've been racked by Civil War, a Great Depression, the Vietnam War, repeated Presidential assassinations, Watergate, 911, and yet we still move forward. Some might say that we're going forward on shaky legs these days, with many of our hallowed principles and institutions under assault and our national strength diminished. Still, there is no other nation like ours on the face of the earth. It saddens me that there are those who are citizens of this great nation who don't see her as being great. It saddens me even more deeply that many deny that God had any special purpose in her birth.

I do believe America is great. In fact, I believe that she is the greatest nation that has ever existed. This nation was built on the backs of immigrants, many of whom came by way of Ellis Island, to the Land of Opportunity. Under the shadow of Lady Liberty, they gazed with wonder at the New World. Sometimes with little more than the clothes on their backs, they forged a life through hard work and determination, so that one day their children, and their children's children, might know a better world than they knew. Many saw this dream become a reality. They were proud to identify as Americans, while never losing the love of the homeland from which they came.

America is different because what makes us Americans is different. We are not bound by a particular ethnicity or common ancestry. Rather, we are bound by a set of propositions which we hold sacred, and to which we adhere. Those propositions are embodied in our Constitution and other founding documents. Yet, it seems that America is more fractured today than ever before. Socially, religiously, racially, and in just about every other way imaginable, Americans are divided, and even, at times, at war with each other. Many, in fact, do not want to even identify as American any more, seeing her as an oppressor of men rather than a liberator, an enemy and tyrant rather than a safe harbor for the world's weary and oppressed. Some would go so far as to say that they see her as a force for evil in the world rather than a force for good.

In reality, America will only ever be what men make her. She can be no better than her citizenry, and only as strong as the commitment of her people to the principles of liberty and democracy. As great as she is, she can be no better than "we the people." The Founders recognized this. Their writings reveal that they were aware that this American experiment could only work if the citizens of this great nation were a moral people, who held themselves accountable to a higher authority than their own personal interests.

A government by the people, no matter how noble its goals and aspirations, can only take us so far. The Bible tells us that man is a fallen being, and as such, he has "self" on the throne of his life. His native North Star is the pursuit and fulfillment of his own interests at whatever cost to others. No common identity will cause us to adhere together as a people if our hearts are darkened by sin. No noble or selfless ideal or purpose can survive if men do not have the power to live noble and selfless lives.

This is why Jesus came: to give us the power to become new. It is only through the transforming power of the gospel that we truly become a new man or woman in Christ, the old, selfish nature replaced by the love of God. He gives us a new identity by making us sons and daughters of God, united by bonds that transcend any natural affiliation or identity. As the scripture says, we "are all one in Christ Jesus."

If there is any people who can erase racial prejudice, it is believers who identify themselves, not merely by their ethnicity, but as part of a heavenly family whose one law is to love one another as He loved us (see John 13:34-35). If there is any people who can erase the hostilities between the sexes, it is those who know that God created us with equal value, yet with complementary strengths that should be embraced and celebrated, rather than despised and rejected. If there is any people that can sit at the table with those with whom we differ and find a solution that transcends personal interest, it is that nation whose God is the Lord, whose people are committed to eternal principles that do not vacillate with the changing winds of culture and man-made ideologies.

All that is good in America is good because it came from God. If you take God out of America, and His rule from our nation, we lose any worthy distinction and will ultimately be torn apart from the inside. No outside enemy poses a threat to our nation like one generation of Americans without godly principles. I love America, but I know that my true identity is in Christ. Only in Him do we share bonds that transcend the evils of this world, and the selfishness of this age. Only in Him do we have the love that is capable of making personal sacrifices for a cause greater than ourselves. Only in Him do I find within me the capacity to love my enemies, or even step outside myself to help a neighbor in need. My identity is in Christ, and it is who I am in Him that can make me a good American.

THE HEAVENS DECLARE

You alone are the Lord;
You have made heaven,
The heaven of heavens, with all their host,
The earth and everything on it,
The seas and all that is in them,
And You preserve them all.
The host of heaven worships You. (Nehemiah 9:6)

It's hard to really wrap one's mind around the enormity of the universe. When one realizes that a single light year is somewhere in the neighborhood of 5.88 trillion miles, and our nearest neighboring star is over four light years, or around 24 trillion miles away, it begins to sink in as to just how truly small we are in the great vastness of the cosmos. The farthest known star from earth is around 13 billion light years away, making one wonder how we even discovered something so distant!

Recent research has suggested that there may be 300 sextillion stars in the known universe, three times as many as previously thought. I have no idea what a *sextillion* is, so I'm no good to you there, but in our own Milky Way Galaxy there are an estimated 300 billion stars, and yet the deep field image from the Hubble telescope shows clusters of galaxies at varying distances, appearing so close together, they look like a dense patch of stars themselves. A 2013 study revealed that there are about 225 billion galaxies in the known universe, and many of them, of course, have as many or more stars in them as does our galaxy.

Numbers like these lose their ability to impact our consciousness, since we have no frame of reference for anything that enormous (which is why we say they're *astronomical*), and even futuristic sci-fi shows like *Star Trek* never presumed to imagine travel outside our own galaxy. Theoretical postulating about wormholes and time travel make great subject matter for movies, such as the recent *Interstellar*, but the laws of physics seem to deny this as being within the realm of reality for us, and present technology can barely take us to our neighboring planets, let alone outside our own solar system.

If our understanding of reality is limited to this physical universe, the seemingly unending space punctuated by stars, nebulae, and the occasional quasar, it all feels vast and very impersonal, even cold and indifferent. It is like an abandoned city, the residents of which seem to have left, leaving the lights on behind them. It is just there, impossibly vast and empty. Yet the Bible teaches us that this universe is not all there is, regardless of its unimaginable size. There is a reality outside space and time that is not subject to the mean laws of nature that bind us to this relatively insignificant planet somewhere on the sidelines of our galaxy. Indeed, it turns out that our place in the universe in not inconsequential at all. The same scriptures seem to teach that our seemingly insignificant world, while not at the physical center of the universe, is the core reason for it all.

In fact, the creation narrative in Genesis is not told from an impersonal context, far removed from us and our world, but as if through the eyes of one who saw it all happen from the front row of planet Earth. Our little planet takes center stage in the universe as God forms man from the dust of the earth, the apex of His creation, made in His image and likeness to experience intimate communion with Him. The very stars and galaxies that we described earlier get only the briefest mention, as they are revealed as the mere backdrop, the distant scenery, in the narrative of God's great story. "…He made the stars also," is the only credit they get in this opening scene to God's great epic (Genesis 1:16).

When the heavens reappear in the Psalms, they are declaring the glory of the Lord and are revealed as His handiwork (Psalm 19:1). When they show up in the New Testament, they are leading the wise men to the One who holds the hopes of men (Matthew 2:1), and at the end of time they will be discarded like old, tattered garments that have served their purpose and must be replaced by new and better clothing. Indeed, the universe as we see it now will pass away, giving way to a new heaven and a new earth (2 Peter 1:13).

While the naturalist claims that the universe somehow brought itself into existence, the Word of God tells a very different story. The Bible teaches us that God spoke the stars into being, and they serve His purpose, displaying His power and revealing His presence to those who look on from down here below. They are given for signs and for seasons, telling us that times are changing and that the fullness of time is rapidly approaching. The heavens have served as our timepiece, and once again there are signs in the heavens telling us that we are in the final hours of this age.

Over the last year, the blood red moons, which appeared once again in conjunction with the three major Jewish feasts, have made big news, inspiring books and many conversations, reminding us of God's uncanny prophetic accuracy (Acts 2:20). We are reminded that all creation obeys God's calendar and declares His purpose and power. So, next time you look into the night sky, don't let yourself feel insignificant. Jesus did not die for those stars. They are but reminders that our God is big enough to reach you where you are and give you a light in the darkness to lead you to the One who gives life and hope to those who look to heaven in faith.

CHANGES

To everything there is a season,

A time for every purpose under heaven. (Ecclesiastes 3:1)

I f there is one thing certain about life, it is change. Take a good look at how things are in your life right now, because they won't be like that for long. Time passes and people move away or pass away. Careers necessitate a change of location and old friends give way to new acquaintances, despite the best intentions to stay in touch. Some changes are easy and even exciting, while others, though inevitable, rip our heart out.

I remember sitting with a couple after a service in our church in New England many years ago. Though originally from the Ivory Coast in Africa, He and his wife had come to us from Belgium where he had gotten his doctorate. He was a research scientist at the University of Vermont, and both he and his wife were beloved members of our church family. When an opportunity came for him to take a position at a University in another state, they both sat with me in the front row while he told me with tears that when their time in this new location was over they would come back. I smiled and told him that would be great, but in my heart I knew it would not happen. Life just isn't like that. It is not static, like a photo. It is more like a river that is fluid, the eddies and currents of which part the best of friends as time and purpose move us in different directions.

They key to life is certainly not in avoiding change. Change is inevitable. In fact, the very nature of this life is transient. We will only be here for a relatively short time. The key to life, rather than avoiding change, is to understand one's purpose. God has a purpose for each and every one of us, and the changing seasons of life are the varied paths we travel in the pursuit and fulfilling of that purpose. The plan of God has literally moved me from one end of the country to another, and even when some of those moves were not as intentional and God-directed as they should have been, God's has always been faithful to bring me to the place where I was supposed to be in His purpose. For some, it is different as they may stay in the same town, or even the same house, all their life long and live a very meaningful and significant life. However, even the most stay-at-home are not immune to change, for it finds us all, wherever we are and wherever we go.

This is why it is always good to appreciate the present season in which we find ourselves. There are relationships we could be enjoying now, rather than always looking around the corner to the next thing coming our way. The future will happen soon enough, but there are things to enjoy in this season which may never come back around in this life. Those of us who have had the opportunity to gain a little perspective remember the years when we were always waiting to be older so we could drive, date, graduate, go to college, or whatever that next exciting thing was that was sure to bring us the fulfillment for which we longed. After arriving at each destination, it seemed the illusive mirage evaporated, leaving us wondering if what we were looking for wasn't perhaps around the next corner. If we could have those years back, knowing what we know now, we wouldn't be in such a hurry. We know now that we simply didn't realize just how good we had it!

Every grandparent tells their children to enjoy their little ones because it won't be long before they are grown and out of the house, and sure enough, time does pass and we're left with the choices we made to either invest in those precious relationships or to neglect them. Indeed, each season, and the choices we make in them, add to the photo album of experiences we collect in this life's journey. Like many family albums in homes today, some are filled with fond memories while others would be better forgotten.

The "Preacher" of Ecclesiastes, said that there is "a time for every purpose under heaven." That means that the time in which we're living right now has a purpose; maybe even several. Our responsibility is to discern what that purpose is and fulfill it, taking every opportunity to invest our time and gifts into those whom God has brought our way, making the most of every opportunity to serve Him. So don't worry about the future. It will come, worry or not, but the people and opportunities you have now may not be present in the next season of your life.

Also, we must learn to let go of regret. Many a good present has been wasted looking back at a less than perfect past. Instead, we must focus our efforts on making the most out of the time we have now. So, invest in your loved ones and friends. Live life well and to the fullest. Work hard, but learn to leave the job behind you at the end of the day, and make room for the people in your life. After all, no one on their death bed wishes they had had another hour to spend at the office.

Add value to others and you will never be wanting for friends. Invest in your children and they will remain close, even if they live far away. Soon this life will be over, and then you will see that it was how you chose to a live each and every today that determined the quality of the life God gave you. There is no way to avoid the pangs that change brings when they separate us from the people and places we love, but knowing that we lived each season well will help us to move confidently into the next stage of the journey, trusting that God is working out His purpose for our lives. As Paul said, "And we know that all things work together for good to those who love God, to those who are the called according to His purpose" (Romans 8:28). God has called you to His purpose. If you love Him and surrender to His call, He will make every changing season become one more layer in the beautiful pattern He is weaving in the fabric of your life.

THE IRREPRESSIBLE GOOD NEWS

Finally, brethren, pray for us, that the word of the Lord may
run swiftly and be glorified, just as it is with you...
(2 Thessalonians 3:1)

Mark Twain was reported to have once humorously quipped,
""A lie can travel halfway around the world while the truth
is putting on its shoes." So it would seem. We know the reality is that
bad news sells, and drama and conflict usually lead to better ratings
than tales of the uneventful happenings in the world. In fact, we are
so inundated with bad news that the occasional "feel good" story at
the end of the evening news is likely to elicit genuine tears as we cling
to the hope that there is still some good in the world.

In reality, there is only good in the world because God is at work
in the world. Were we to be bereft of his presence and the hope that
we have in Christ, there would indeed be no cause for rejoicing anywhere. Apart from the good news of the gospel, man can only look
forward to the certainty of judgment. The buildup to the end of all
things has begun, and we who live in this time are truly witnesses
to history in the making. For many, this will be a time of terror and
fear, but to those who hope in Christ, it is the time in which we are

told to lift our heads in anticipation for our redemption (see Luke 21:25-28). For those who have eyes to see and ears to hear, the cryptic prophecies made by Old Testament prophets are coming to pass with chilling accuracy before our very eyes, from the realization of the nation of Israel reassembling like so many dry bones in their ancient homeland, to the blood red moons Joel predicted hundreds of years before Christ walked the earth. These things are given as a witness, not only to the fulfillment of God's end time plan, but as proof to the credibility of the witness of scripture.

When one considers that the sixty-six books of the Bible were penned by more than forty authors over a period of roughly fifteen hundred years, the coherency and unity of the message are incredible. In Isaiah, chapter 53, we see the shadowy prefiguring of the suffering Servant, while in the gospels we see the blood-red reality of His crucifixion. In Numbers we see Moses lift up the brazen serpent so that all who are bitten in the camp may be healed, while on the cross we see the anti-type of that image raised up so that all who look upon Him might be saved. We see in the Exodus the bleeding of the Passover lamb, the innocent suffering for the guilty, while at Calvary we see the Lamb of God taking away the sins of the world. All the images, sacrifices, and prophetic writings testify to redemption's story, of God coming down to earth that the way to heaven may be opened for sinful men.

For generations the greatest story ever told has crossed the seas, leapt over walls, passed through barbed wire, and slipped through borders to lift the hearts of the oppressed, give strength to the faint, and restore sight to the blind. That story of redemption inspired Handel to write his *Messiah* and moved Michelangelo, Dante, and countless others to create their immortal masterpieces of art and verse. More than any other figure in human history, the looming figure of the Son of Man has ennobled men, delivered captives, lifted the lowly, and given hope in the midst of hopelessness. While His detractors have been many, he has outlived them all to remain the most influential figure in all the world. Countless faithful believers, willingly to pay the ultimate price, have suffered persecution and even perished while carrying this imperishable message of good news to the lost. Still today many suffer as they worship God and His Son, Jesus, whom He sent to save us all. They do so because they know their hope will outlive this life here below, and that their ultimate reward is awaiting them in eternity.

This is a living word that no man, government, or ideology can stop, and indeed, as Christ declared, the gates of hell have been unable to prevail against His Church. The scriptures testify to that Kingdom yet to come to earth, and which has already come to dwell in the hearts of believers. It is a Kingdom that cannot be assailed or conquered, whose King has already triumphed over His foes. It is a Kingdom into which all may freely enter, but into which we can only find access under the shadow of the cross. This Kingdom has no address and yet it can be found on every continent and every nation, while its ambassadors run to carry its message of emancipation from the bondage of sin to wherever men are found. This is the good news that through Christ our captivity has been turned, and the way to tree of life has been reopened.

If you are reading this, that message has now come to you. The gospel is not a call to better or reform oneself through personal effort or religious ceremony, but to surrender all attempts to earn God's favor and simply trust in the Savior who paid our debt and made forgiveness and salvation available. God's desire is for you to not only receive this new life for yourself but to become a Kingdom carrier, sharing in both word and deed the reality of the transformative power of the gospel with those whose hearts are hungry for the eternal realities of peace with God and purpose for life. In doing so, you become part of that living story that continues to change lives today, from the remotest jungles of Central America to the skyscrapers of Manhattan, from the Sub-Saharan deserts of Africa to the marbled halls of power.

It is easy to become pessimistic, cynical, and even despondent as we see the terrible things that are happening in the world. Indeed, there is great darkness in many places, but we do not lose heart as though God has gone out of business. He is at work in the world today, and the gospel is still finding an audience in the hearts of men. One day the tattered curtain of space and time will fall away, and we will step into that eternal reality which is our great hope, and from which we will never depart. Until then, we who believe can know that just on the other side of that veil are the millions of believers who have preceded us into glory, cheering us on as we take the irrepressible good news of Jesus to the ends of the earth.

A FOOL'S TALE

The fool has said in his heart,

"There is no God."

They are corrupt, and have done abominable iniquity;

There is none who does good.

God looks down from heaven upon the children of men,

To see if there are any who understand, who seek God.

Every one of them has turned aside;

They have together become corrupt;

There is none who does good,

No, not one. (Psalm 53:1-3)

If I were the devil, I would do exactly what the devil has sought to do in our society: make Christianity seem like a foolish children's story, believed only by those who have failed to wake up to the realities of modern life and the "hard realities" of science. I would have talk show hosts, like Bill Maher, make fun of and belittle Christians openly, inviting as guests some of the more popular entertainment personalities to serve as either foils or accomplices in his attempts to ridicule the biblical narrative.

Furthermore, I would do as he has done in the halls of higher education and have henchmen like Richard Dawkins, former Oxford don and author of the wildly popular book, *The God Delusion*, openly deride people of faith and encourage others to do the same. I would have those who espouse a materialistic worldview (meaning that our universe is nothing more than a product of matter, plus time, plus chance) intimidate those in the academy with a biblical worldview, so as to shame them into being silent or risk being perceived as naïve and intellectually inferior.

I would have our society espouse a tolerance that borders on total permissiveness, tossing aside all former definitions of right and wrong and good and evil. In fact, the only taboo would be for anyone to hold on to antiquated conventions that dared to challenge another's behavior by calling it "sinful" or, even worse, "ungodly." I would endeavor to have those who held to their religious convictions to be labeled as the new bigots of our society, who want nothing more than to stanch the true self-expression of others while holding on to a hypocritical sense of their own moral superiority.

If this sounds familiar to anyone, it is because it is the direction in which our culture is moving. This should not surprise us, since Satan is called "the god of this world" (2 Corinthians 4:4), and the "prince of the power of the air" who steers the course of this world through "the desires of the flesh and of the mind" (Ephesians 2:1-3). His influence can certainly be felt in every sector of society from our educational institutions, to the marketplace, to our halls of government, and even more grievously, in some of our churches. Those who desire to shed the "restrictive" cords of biblical Christianity laud this progressive secularization of our society, wanting only to be happily free from absolutes, free from restrictions, free from God.

This is all well and good for the secularist, unless, of course, there *is* a God. If there is a God, as the Bible declares, then there is an objective, moral Lawgiver who has drawn definite, immutable lines of right and wrong as the scriptures teach, and to Whom all men are accountable. If there is a God, then He has given evidence of Himself, not only in the myriad of Bible prophecies that have come to pass with chilling accuracy, but in the very universe itself, which declares the glory of God and upon which His divine fingerprints can be clearly seen. If there is a God, then the many qualified scientists who have found evidence of intelligent design in both the macro as well as the micro worlds of scientific exploration need not feel bullied by the less convincing arguments of a dead Darwinism that has long ceased to hold up in the light of more recent discoveries.

More than all this, if there is a God, then it is neither bigoted nor narrow-minded to say that God's righteousness does not reconcile itself to all the willful ways of men. It is, in point of fact, love of the highest degree to risk being marginalized and maligned to point out that man is sinful, desperately wicked, and unable to save himself. Only a calloused and loveless person could watch so many heading blindly to the brink of destruction and not sound an alarm, warning that the boundaries God has drawn are not intended to be restrictive as such, but rather protective and even instructive. God's law not only gives us a template of justice upon which to base our society, but it also reveals a standard of righteousness only possible through the redeeming work of Christ wrought in the human heart. That salvation is found in Jesus alone. In fact, the scriptures boldly declare that there is salvation in no other (see Acts 4:12, John 14:6). This is not a righteousness any government can legislate or any system of religion can impute through the keeping of rules, but one which comes only by an unfathomable wellspring of grace, purchased by the greatest sacrifice the world has ever known.

Needless to say, this idea of man's dependence upon a transcendent God for his salvation does not sit well with everyone, least of all those who are fighting hard to keep their moral autonomy. In fact, the scriptures declare that, "the message of the cross is foolishness to those who are perishing, but to us who are being saved it is the power of God" (1 Corinthians 1:18). To the world our faith may be but a fool's tale, but to us who have unlocked the gospel's power through faith, it is the message of life abundant, life eternal. So, it seems to me that we can either reject the wisdom of this world and be regarded a fool in the eyes of men for the gospel's sake, or keep to our own wisdom, rejecting the mercy and benevolence of a loving God, and be a fool as the scriptures describe.

In 1 Corinthians 1:19, Paul quotes from an Old Testament passage in Isaiah, in which God says, "I will destroy the wisdom of the wise, and bring to nothing the understanding of the prudent." God is going to have the last word in this great debate. At that time there will be no bravado, no counterpoint, no pithy comebacks, and no smugness. There will be only two groups of people on that day: those who chose what seemed a fool's tale and those who were truly foolish in dismissing the salvation offered through the grace of God in Christ Jesus.

THE DEFINITE ARTICLE

Jesus told him, "I am the way, the truth, and the life. No one can come to the Father except through me." (John 14:6)

To be certain, Jesus is the real deal. No believer in Christ would dispute that. But in using the phrase, "the definite article," I do not mean it as merely another way of saying that Jesus is *authentic*. In fact, I mean it in a more practical, even grammatical way. When Jesus spoke of Himself, as recorded in the verse above, He used the definite article, "THE". He is THE way, THE truth, and THE life. Let me tell you, "THE" will mess you up, especially if you have been conditioned by our culture's homogenized brand of political correctness and moral relativism to believe that "all views are true" and "every path leads to God."

That definite article claims a very particular uniqueness to Christ. If He is THE way, then Muhammad is not. If Jesus is THE truth, then Buddha is not. If Jesus is THE exclusive way to the Father, which He emphatically affirmed, then modern society's fantasy about truth being relative has just been turned on its head. Jesus obviously would not have fared well with the modern purveyors of political, cultural, and social correctness that are ready to intimidate anyone who dares to utter an opinion that does not fit their morally relative, socially and politically progressive narrative.

But the real fact of the matter is that all truth claims are, by their very nature, exclusive. You cannot say that two opposing ideas are equally true (unless you're a politician). If a proponent of one ideology claims his to be true, then he is, by implication, saying that any ideology that holds an opposing view is wrong. The fact is, not all religions are created equal, nor can they all, by any logical analysis, be true. How could they be when they each hold to their own distinctive doctrines, so radically different from one another in almost every essential way? Obviously, not all truth claims are, in fact, true. The idea that all religions are "essentially the same" is pure fallacy. But, as Jesus declared, there is a truth that is knowable. There is in all of this, a right answer, and contrary to popular sentiment, if one's particular beliefs are opposed to that truth, then those beliefs are wrong. That's right, my friend. Wrong.

These kinds of direct assertions of truth are very difficult for our culture to hear today. Maybe even difficult enough to send some overly sensitive university students running back shrieking to their safe zones! In fact, any opinion expressed as definitively true sends a hoard of folks howling about the insensitivity of such truth claims to those who don't share those views. Where did this hypersensitivity come from? We are so worried about political correctness in our culture that we can't say anything that means anything anymore. We can't say that most acts of terror are being carried out by radical Islamic jihadists, lest we offend our Muslim neighbors. Of course we're not saying that all Muslims are terrorists. They are not, but we should not unsay, or leave unsaid, what is patently true for fear of offending a particular group. We cannot say that violent rioting and looting in our inner cities is wrong lest we be said to be insensitive to the plight of minorities who feel that they have been oppressed by authority figures in our society. It is the Constitutionally protected right of every American citizen to make such claims, and there are proper legal channels by which such wrongs may be addressed and justice served. However, while those who riot cry out for fair treatment, they ignore the rights of the innocent citizens whose businesses are destroyed in the name of their demonstrations for justice.

We are prohibited by political correctness from saying that killing an unborn child in the womb of its mother is murder and the greatest shame in our national history, lest we be accused of trampling the rights of women. Such words would be considered an attack on those young girls who are in a vulnerable position in life, and yet little is said by the talking heads in our culture about the sheer inhumanity of selling the fetal remains of the unborn for profit, even though they, the *most* vulnerable among us, are denied the most basic of rights: the right to life.

It would seem that saying anything could be potentially offensive to someone somewhere. In fact, in recent news, students on the campus of Yale University were signing a petition to rescind the First Amendment on the grounds that it promotes "hate speech." When exactly did the world go nuts? When did the lunatics take over the asylum? I am not exactly sure when it happened, but happen it did. No one is allowed to express opinions that are too direct, or espouse values as being absolutely true, because somewhere along the line our society decided that right and wrong were negotiable, and that truth was whatever an individual wanted it to be based on their feelings, wants, and needs.

There is, however, one big problem with all of this. We are not the ultimate arbiters of what is right and wrong. Before any of us came on the scene, objective truth was already set down by the One who just as meticulously established the laws of physics that allow our world to spin its way through the cosmos. It will not be a secularist or moral relativist before whom we stand when we are called upon to give an account of ourselves. Our feeble attempts to redefine the nonnegotiable will not wash before the One who is Himself the embodiment of truth.

That One sent His Son to die for our sins. He did not make it complicated. He gave us in the scriptures the necessary revelation of Himself so that the big questions of life could be an open book test. In whom can we put our trust? Where is truth to be found upon which we can build our lives? Where is meaning found that makes sense of why we were born? Against the panoply of pretenders stands One whose birth split time in half, BC and AD, and whose life has done more to influence the course of human history than any other. His name is Jesus, and He is, quite literally, the answer, the *definite article!*

The tactic to get our world to deny absolutes was not merely the invention of men who wanted to justify their selfish ambitions and defend their carnal pursuits. This is no mere concoction of a culture that simply wants to do its own thing. This strategy was conceived in hell by Satan, the "god of this world," who blinds the minds of those "who do not believe, lest the light of the gospel of the glory of Christ, who is the image of God, should shine on them" (2 Corinthians 4:4). He distracts men from their hunger for truth with the lures of desire, pride, and selfish ambition. He lulls them into stupefaction with witty sounding arguments from the atheistic intelligentsia who tell them that the moral conventions of our fathers' faith are outdated and passé. Those seeking to ignore the warning of their conscience take this as their permission slip to skip out on the serious conversation about truth, moral accountability, and eternal destiny.

The fact is that time is short. It is time to take a stand, choose a side, and get…*definite!* We need to be definite about what we believe, in whom we trust, and on what we'll stake our lives. This is much too important an issue for the truth to be lost or diluted in ambiguous terms that don't mean anything, simply because we want to be "nice" and "inclusive" and "polite" about it all. We don't want to offend anyone, but neither do we want to entertain falsehood so everyone can merely feel better about themselves. We won't all agree. Some whom we dearly love may disagree with us the most adamantly. We will still love them, and respect their right to dissent, but we have a higher obligation to the truth, for when we deny the truth we ourselves participate in deception.

As C. S. Lewis once famously explained, we cannot see Jesus merely as a good man or a teacher of great truths. He did not leave us that option. He claimed to be the Messiah, the Son of the living God. He is either liar, lunatic, or Lord. He gave us the answer when He said He was the way, the truth, and the life. You must choose whom you will believe. You need to make an informed decision. This is too important to leave to others to decide for you. This is indeed something about which you need to be definite.

A CRISIS OF INFINITESIMAL PROPORTIONS

Blind guides, who strain out a gnat and swallow a camel!
(Matthew 23:24)

Have you ever been caught doing something that was innocent enough in itself, yet you still felt the need to explain yourself? If you haven't, let me share with you my most recent such experience. I wanted honey, but the large Costco-sized container of honey was full of a somewhat cloudy version of the contents, as it had begun to crystalize into sugar. My solution was to place the whole thing into the microwave to let it melt down enough to get some out of the container and continue the melting process with the smaller amount I needed. It sounded fine when I initially ran the plan through my head, but when my stepson suddenly came into the kitchen in the middle of my honey extracting efforts with a quizzical look, I began to feel the need to explain myself. After casting a dubious look at the whole operation, he laughed and said, "Definitely a first world problem!"

I had to laugh at the absurdity of the situation. It was true. In much of the world the challenge merely to survive is enough to occupy one's entire day. I recently read a story of an orphanage opened up in Kenya by a missionary who had experienced seeing children rummage through the giant mounds of trash to find food and then cook it on a makeshift campfire. What wouldn't they give to have the trouble of getting a little honey for their meal out of a giant commercial-sized container bought at the local wholesale food store as their biggest challenge?

It is true that due to the prosperity and modern conveniences we enjoy in the West, we have been shielded, to a great degree, from many of the harsh realities others face in developing parts of the world. As a consequence, things that would not even register on their radar as a need become all-consuming for us, such as when we can't find the sporting event we want to watch on the hundred or more television channels we have at our fingertips. We can make much ado out of what is, in reality, nothing at all. Certainly, there are exceptions to this, such as when someone we love is diagnosed with a serious illness or we experience a layoff or setback, but compared to much of the world, our perception of what makes life challenging is often really nothing.

This is not only true in the context of how we perceive what constitutes a challenge in our modern lives, but also in how we relate to one another and carry out the business of the Kingdom of God. In the days of the early Church, believers' lives were on the line every day. When Paul told Timothy that "God has not given us a spirit of fear, but of power and of love and of a sound mind," it was not because Timothy was nervous about preaching his first message in front of the home crowd, but because the next message he preached could very well be his last. Paul himself bid Timothy farewell at the end of this,

his last epistle, noting that the time of his martyrdom was at hand. Timothy would later experience the same fate, following his spiritual father in paying the ultimate price for his devotion to the Lord.

In the foxhole, petty differences are put aside and soldiers work together for the common goal of winning the war for their country. What may have been an issue of division in the luxury of peacetime is not even noticed in the light of the larger, looming demands for which they must rely upon one another. It is in the furnace of such trials that the deepest alliances are made, and such friendships often transcend race, culture, or any other natural barrier, to last a lifetime. Perhaps our tendency to maximize the minimal and make mountains out of molehills is a result of our failure to recognize the greater overarching issues we as the Church of Jesus Christ are faced with in our time.

We are often too comfortable in our comfort to be troubled with real troubles, so we become purveyors of the petty. What else can explain churches being split over non-issues, such as carpet colors and worship styles? How is it that we will sever ties with fellow believers over doctrinal issues that have no bearing whatsoever on the weightier matters of the faith or over insignificant personal differences in church? Many offenses are nothing more than perceived wrongs because someone allowed their imagination to be the Devil's playground. It has become about us and our interests rather than laying down our lives for one another and the interests of the Kingdom.

Whatever else may be true, until we make the main thing the main thing, we will always allow the real issues we should be focused on to be usurped by non-essential nonsense. Jesus addressed this with the Pharisees when He rebuked them for giving great attention to the minutia of the law but omitting the weightier matters of "justice, mercy, and faith" (see Matthew 23:23). Because they obsessed over the wrong things, putting their focus on themselves, their own self-righteousness, and their rule-keeping rather than true holiness, their ability to see what was truly important was impaired. Jesus called them "blind guides."

I have spent my life around the Church and seen many sad scenarios of infighting and division started by nothing more than a person's desire to have things run their own way, not concerned at all that their energies were completely misdirected from the purpose for which the church existed in the first place. They were completely blinded to the real issues and opportunities for service around them because they were consumed with what wouldn't even pass for a concern were their priorities in the right place. We need to realize that we have allowed first world issues to consume us in the Church, and this has weakened our ability to tackle real issues and focus on the bigger picture of reaching our world for Christ. What's more, we have picked a bad time to do so. Never before has our nation been in such dire need of a united Church with a clear vision and an unremitting commitment to see it through.

Not every issue is worth dying on the field of battle for. In fact, most are certainly not. The Church must rise above petty bickering and sectarian differences and unite over what really matters. We have plenty to learn from one another, and where one of us is weak we can benefit from the other's strength. The Devil knows this, and seeks to keep us from locking arms and marching together in unbroken rank for the purposes of God.

The gates of hell cannot prevail against the Church, but divided believers are easy prey. It is worth asking ourselves if the thing that is keeping us from joining hands with our brothers and sisters is really worth the price others will have to pay for our pettiness. It's not a comfortable question, because it is one for which we know the answer all too well. Who will be the bigger man or woman, who will set aside their wants, their needs, and even their life for the Kingdom of God? That is the person who will change the world.

BLANK

Therefore, if anyone is in Christ, he is a new creation; old things have passed away; behold, all things have become new. (2 Corinthians 5:17)

It's not often that I'm short of inspiration when it comes to writing, but every once in a while, as is common with those frequently engaged in creative endeavors, I draw a blank. It was, in fact, while looking at the virtual blank page on my Mac version of Microsoft Word that inspiration struck. What is *blank* if not a perfect place to start? From blank you can say anything, go anywhere, or do anything. Blank holds limitless potential and is wholly unspoiled. Every new day is a blank page on which to write a new story, every new opportunity a blank canvas on which to paint a new masterpiece of experience, and every new life a blank slate upon which a new story will be written.

There are plenty of people in the world that would give anything just to get back to blank. The harsh realities of life from which they have suffered have etched deep wounds on the tablet of their heart from which they have not yet healed. For others, bad choices have scrawled a story of failure in the mind which they cannot forget; their confidence crippled and their hearts filled with guilt. Sometimes you can see eyes filled with the weariness of a life without purpose, without hope, and without direction; eyes which reflect the futility they feel deep in their soul. What wouldn't these give to have their slate cleared, their history deleted, and their past erased, just to get back to blank?

Where can one find a new beginning when already years into life's race? How can one who has seen too much of the ugly side of life recover their innocence? How can one find a second chance to live a life of meaning and purpose rather than of regret? It's not possible from a human standpoint. No one can rewrite the past or undo the thing that was done or unsay the hurtful thing said. No one can back up to yesterday and say what should have been said or do a retake on the opportunity squandered. But what if you could? What if you could go back? What if there was a sponge that could wipe away the problem, the pain, and the past? What if you could be born again?

The good news is that God specializes in do-overs. In fact, since the Garden of Eden, God has been on a restoration project with the entire human race. No, God did not remove the teeth marks of Adam in the forbidden fruit, but He did have a salvage plan in place; a contingency in the light of what He, in His omniscience, knew would be the inevitable failure of mankind. He didn't take Adam back to the day before he disobeyed God's only prohibition in paradise, for that would be one and the same as taking from Adam the right to choose in the first place. He couldn't "undo" what Adam did, but what He could do was to provide another Adam.

Jesus, the last Adam, came and passed the tests the first Adam failed. Not only that, but He paid the price for the first Adam's failure by serving as his substitute on the cross, and since we were all "in Adam," so to speak, when he made that dreadful choice in the Garden, Jesus served as our substitute as well. He did all of this for one reason, to get us back to blank. He did it to erase the record of our sin and failure before the Judgement Seat of God, and provide an acquittal of our guilt.

Now, when anyone accepts what Christ did for them, and receives the free gift of new life God offers through Him, his old life becomes a blank. As the apostle Paul said, "If anyone is in Christ, he is a new creation: old things have passed away." But it gets even better, because God draws a new image on the tablet of our heart. In place of the old image of guilt, inadequacy, and failure, He paints a new picture of forgiveness, reconciliation, and righteousness. Better still is the fact that this new image is written in the indelible ink of the blood of Christ, who died that the book of our life could be rewritten. "Therefore, if anyone is in Christ, he is a new creation; old things have passed away; behold, all things have become new" (2 Corinthians 5:17).

You can be born again. In fact, Jesus said we *must* be born again if we are to discover this new life in Him (John 3:3). The cross is the intersection at which we part with our poorly written past, and turn the pen over to the one who will write the new story of our life. It is a story with a "happily ever after," but it's also a story written, not only for us, but for all the others who are desperate to believe that their story can be rewritten too.

BELIEVING IS PERCEIVING

For as he thinks in his heart, so is he. (Proverbs 23:7)

What you perceive to be true becomes the reality in which you live. This is not meant to be some deep, metaphysical statement. It's simply the truth. We've all known people who were kind, wonderful people who lived very insecure lives simply because they believed something untrue about themselves. Maybe you are one of those people.

What you choose to believe will, without a doubt, determine the quality of your life. If you believe you're unlovely, unwanted, and unwelcomed, you will live life looking down at the ground, afraid to make eye contact with people. If you believe you are a person who has the ability to add value to others, you will likely be confident and outgoing, looking for opportunities to encourage and invest in people. This principle is not only true naturally, it's true spiritually as well. What we believe shapes our perceptions, and our perceptions shape the reality in which we live.

When it comes to your own personal value, you have to decide who you are going to believe. You may have had parents or peers who failed to value you. You may have been made to feel worthless to those around you, but the fact is, no man, woman, boy, or girl has either the right or the power to determine your value. In fact, your value has already been determined by the cost God was willing to pay, and the length He was willing to go, to secure your redemption, "knowing that you were not redeemed with corruptible things, like silver or gold… but with the precious blood of Christ, as of a lamb without blemish and without spot" (1 Peter 1:18-19).

If the value of a thing is determined by the price paid for it, then you and I are of inestimable worth to God. He placed a value on us above all the wealth of this world when He spilled the blood of His Son to secure our pardon – to redeem us back to Himself. If I were to offer a one-hundred-dollar bill to a crowd of people and said, "This bill has been used in strip clubs, drug deals, and illegal arms sales," I bet I would still have a lot of takers. Why? Because where that bill has been and how it has been used does nothing to take away from its inherent worth. Likewise, regardless of where one has been or what he or she has done, it does nothing to reduce their inherent worth to God. He paid the same price for the prince as He did the prostitute.

In Christ we are given a new identity. In fact, Paul said, "Therefore, if anyone is in Christ, he is a new creation; old things have passed away; behold, all things have become new" (2 Corinthians 5:17). God does not see us as an "old sinner," but as one whom He has declared righteous through the redeeming work of Christ (see 2 Corinthians 5:21). In fact, the Bible says that if we have accepted Jesus as Lord and Savior, we are "in Christ," meaning that our identity is lost in Him. He does not see us as we once were, but in the light of that redemption: forgiven, cleansed, and worthy to stand in His presence, not by virtue of our own works, but because of the finished work of Christ. What we must do is believe that, for what we believe will determine our perception, and our perception will shape the reality in which we live. Too many believers are living defeated lives simply because they refuse to believe what God says about them in the light of the redemption He secured on their behalf.

Let me remind you for a moment regarding what God says about you, the child of God. The Bible says that He has delivered you from the power of darkness (Colossians 1:13) and seated you together with Him in heavenly places in Christ (Ephesians 2:6), which is far above all demonic principalities and powers (Ephesians 1:19-21). God has qualified you through Christ to be His child, and He has given you an inheritance among all His saints (Colossians 1:12). He has put His Spirit within you to reveal His secrets to your heart (1 Corinthians 2:12), and that same Spirit lives in you forever, as your constant companion, helper, and guide, and He will even show you things to come (John 16:13). There is no need you will ever have for which God has not already made provision (2 Peter 1:2-4), and all His promises to you are sure (2 Corinthians 1:20). God loves you, and He invites you to come boldly to His throne of grace to enjoy rich fellowship with Him, as well as to obtain mercy and find grace to help in your time of need (Hebrews 4:15-16).

There is more, much more, that God says about you, but it will not benefit your life unless you believe it. If you believe the things that God says about you, you will live an empowered, victorious, and fruitful life. If you believe what the devil whispers in your ear about you, you will live in frustration and defeat, even though God has already blessed you with "every spiritual blessing in heavenly places in Christ" (Ephesians 1:3).

Many years ago, I knew a man who attended a church I pastored who seemed to really struggle in his Christian walk. When he was in fellowship, there was no one who worked harder to serve in the church. When he was "out" we wouldn't see him for months. One Sunday in church, he testified about an experience he had that I believe illustrates the power of perception as much as anything I have ever heard. He said that he had a dream in which he was looking through prison bars at a horrible being he knew to be Satan. The Devil was laughing and mocking him as he looked at him through those prison bars. As he was feeling the horror and oppression of his apparent situation, he heard behind him a voice that called his name. When he turned and looked around, he saw that he was not behind bars at all, but rather standing in a beautiful, green field. Jesus was standing there with His arms opened to him. It had been He who had called his name. Suddenly, this man looked back to see that it was, in fact, the devil behind those bars, while he stood free and in the presence of Jesus Himself. The difference between freedom and bondage for the child of God is determined by whether or not we truly believe in what Christ has done for us. Are we looking to the lies of the devil, or the liberating truths of God's Word?

"If the Son makes you free, you shall be free indeed" (John 8:36). You have been made free, righteous, and holy by the sanctifying work of Christ. As your mind is renewed to the reality of who you are in Him, and what He has provided for you, you will begin to rise to new heights in your walk and relationship with the Lord and enjoy a fruitful and fulfilling life. If you have not yet accepted Christ, His hand is stretched out still. The price has already been paid and the table set. There is a place for you there if you will but accept His gracious invitation.

TRANSCENDENCE

Of old You laid the foundation of the earth,
And the heavens are the work of Your hands.
They will perish, but You will endure;
Yes, they will all grow old like a garment;
Like a cloak You will change them,
And they will be changed.
But You are the same,
And Your years will have no end.
(Psalm 102:25-27)

The greatest cosmological discovery of the twentieth century was possibly the discovery of the finite universe. Before Edwin Hubble discovered "Hubble's Law," which empirically confirmed that our universe was expanding, science regarded the universe to be static and eternal. This was known as the *Steady State Model* of the universe. However, the logical conclusion of reverse engineering Hubble's Law is that if the universe is expanding, then at one point in time it had to have had a beginning. Thus, with the observable evidence of Hubble's law corroborating Einstein's theory of General Relativity, the undeniable conclusion that our universe had a beginning came crashing down on the scientific community like the proverbial ton of bricks.

The implications were colossal. If the universe had a beginning, then that means it had a *cause*, for as the *Kalum Cosmological Argument* contends, "Anything that *begins* to exist, must have a cause." Thus the *Big Bang Model* of the universe came into the scientific lexicon, and it has over time become the accepted scientific paradigm to explain the origin of the universe. However, this presented an enormous problem for the materialists (those who believe there is nothing outside of the material universe). If all mater, energy, space, and time came into existence at the moment of the Big Bang, then none of those things can used in the explanation of that cause. Thus, the logical conclusion was that there had to be a transcendent, immaterial, eternal, intelligent, all-powerful causal Agent who got the whole thing going.

Forty percent of scientists today are theists, meaning that they acknowledge there is some intelligent Designer behind the creation of our universe. Why do they believe this? Simple! The science leaves no room for any other reasonable answer. The fine tuning of the universe, along with a host of other factors, is so incredibly precise as to defy any possibility of randomness or chance. In fact, the evidence of the fine tuning of the universe led famous English astronomer, Sir Fred Hoyle, to say, "A commonsense interpretation of the facts suggests that a superintellect has monkeyed with physics, as well as chemistry and biology, and that there are no blind forces worth speaking about in nature. The numbers one calculates from the facts seem to me so overwhelming as to put this conclusion almost beyond question."[7]

The evidence to support Hoyle's conclusion has only grown in recent years. In short, science is more in favor now of what is popularly called the *God Hypothesis* than ever before. Of course, what has taken scientists years of observing a huge and expanding preponderance of evidence to acknowledge, the Bible has declared from the beginning. The Bible says, with no apology and without regard to the doubts of Darwinists, "In the beginning God created the heavens and the earth" (Genesis 1:1). That means before everything that we can observe through our telescopes was created, God was there. Before there was matter, energy, space, or time, God *was*. That's hard to wrap our minds around. It is hard to conceive of the eternality of God. It's not like God has been around for a long, long time. Rather, He sits outside of time and is wholly unaffected by it. That is what we call *transcendence*. He is above and beyond…everything. He is independent, outside of His creation: eternal, immutable, omniscient, omnipresent, and omnipotent.

In verses like the Psalm quoted at the beginning of this article, the Bible reveals to us God's transcendence, and in doing so, testifies to its own credibility. After all, if the writers of scripture were making all this up, they would have invented a God that would have been easier to comprehend, like the Greeks and Romans did. They worshipped gods who behaved much more like us with their conniving and capricious behavior, or, in other words, gods made in our image rather than the other way around. Instead, the Bible describes certain characteristics about God, such as His triune nature, that have puzzled and perplexed the brightest of minds for centuries. However, instead of undermining the case for the Creator, these difficult aspects of His Being described in the scriptures serve rather to authenticate their account of His existence. After all, if we are talking about a God who spoke billions of light years of universe into existence and sustains it all without so much as breaking a sweat, we should hope that He defies easy explanation. Nevertheless, He reveals enough about Himself to us that we might begin to comprehend His majesty and understand His nature.

The very fact that He reveals Himself at all tells us something more about Him. He wants to be known. The Bible itself claims to be an inspired transmission to us from God, given that we might understand Him, and ultimately, come to know Him (see 2 Timothy 3:16-17 & 2 Peter 1:20-21). These scriptures do not merely reveal a God of power and genius, but one who is relational. In fact, while science can begin to explain certain aspects of the physical creation to us, it can never answer the more important question, "Why did God make it all in the first place?"

The Genesis story of creation is not told from the perspective of the physical center of the universe, but rather from the vantage point of the earth, a seemingly insignificant planet, orbiting an average star in an unremarkable part of our galaxy (one among an estimated five hundred billion galaxies, by the way). Yet, it was on this planet that the story of God and man took place, a story with many chapters, filled with sorrow and death, but also of redemption and hope. It's a masterful story in which we all play a central part as the objects of God's love. In fact, because He is transcendent, He saw you and I coming a long way off and made provision for us to be reconciled to Him, even before we ate the forbidden fruit that caused us to lose our place in paradise. In the end, it's a story of two trees: one where we fell, and one where He raised us up. The one in the Garden was where we died, but the one on Calvary was where His Son died, that we might be reconciled to Him.

None of the billions of stars in all the billions of galaxies are as important as those three rusty nails and that old rugged cross, for it was there, at Calvary, that God's grace met our need. It was there that the transcendent, eternal Creator of the universe entered time and space to become one of us, that we might become one with Him.

ONE MAN

Therefore just as through the trespass of ONE MAN came condemnation for all men, so through the righteous act of One came justification of life for all men. (Romans 5:18 *Modern English Version, emphasis mine*)

Can one man really change the world? I would argue that this verse alone testifies to the fact that, on at least two separate occasions, one man *did* change the world. God placed man in Paradise, and yet through Adam's disobedience we were alienated from our Creator and exiled from peace and perfection. Since Adam was our representative in the Garden, he not only chose for himself, but for us as well. That one choice forever changed the world. I don't know exactly what life would have been like today had the Tree of the Knowledge of Good and Evil and its forbidden fruit been left alone, but I do know that due to that one man's disobedience, mankind was plunged into a world of cruelty, violence, and death through the fallen nature we inherited.

However, as we know, that is not the end of the story, for Christ came as the *last Adam* (see 1 Corinthians 15:19); one Man to represent us once again, this time on an old rugged cross on a Judean hillside, just outside of Jerusalem. There the sins of mankind were paid in full and the scales of divine justice balanced on our behalf. Now, instead of being driven from the presence of God, the temple veil that represented the separation between the holy and the sinful, the pure from the profane, was rent from the top to the bottom, showing that God had reopened our way to Him through Christ's sacrifice. Again, one Man changed the world.

Of course, Jesus was different. His supernatural origin and virgin birth meant that He was not tainted with the sin nature into which each of us is born. He was God made flesh (John 1:14), and we are not. Only He could change the world in *that* way, and yet, there is no question that He has commissioned and empowered the Church to continue His work in the earth through the proclamation of the gospel. He said Himself that we would do His works and even greater (see John 14:12). Besides, I would argue that there are other men who have so singularly impacted the generation into which they were born that one could say they *changed* the world. The Apostle Paul, Martin Luther, William Wilberforce, and others we could name, left such an indelible mark on the world in which they lived that life for those born afterward was different; the course of human events altered by their contribution, and through it they still influence our lives today. However, others changed the world too. Marx, Lenin, and Hitler likewise left their mark on history, and the world is still reeling from the horrors their names and deeds recall. As with Adam and Jesus, men—for good or ill—still change the world.

The verse above says that "one man" changed the lives of "all men." Adam did it. Jesus did it. Others have done it to some extent. In fact, the eleventh chapter of the epistle to the Hebrews is full of the names of men and women who changed the world in which they lived. Noah, Abraham, and Moses, just to name a few, are famous in the pantheon of biblical heroes who changed the world because they were driven, at any cost, by a heavenly vision.

We too are called to run our race with endurance that the world in which we live might likewise experience the life, character, and power of God (see Hebrews 12:1). The fact is, all of us will leave our mark on the world in some way. Whether that change is good or evil will depend upon the people we choose to become and our willingness to be intentional about pursuing God's purpose for our lives, and the price we're willing to pay to see it through. Our culture has become self-absorbed, and too few are looking for a larger, more worthy cause in which to invest themselves. Yet, our lives are like a seed. Planted in the right soil, it has great potential. Left alone, it produces nothing.

> But Jesus answered them, saying, "The hour has come that the Son of Man should be glorified. Most assuredly, I say to you, unless a grain of wheat falls into the ground and dies, it remains alone; but if it dies, it produces much grain. He who loves his life will lose it, and he who hates his life in this world will keep it for eternal life. If anyone serves Me, let him follow Me; and where I am, there My servant will be also. If anyone serves Me, him My Father will honor." (John 12:23-26)

Changing the world cost Jesus His life. I imagine, if you could speak to Paul, Luther, or Wilberforce today, they would tell you that in a very real way, serving God's purpose in their respective lives cost them theirs as well. Their reward is both in heaven and in the return their investment produced in the world. And yet, these men should not to be unique in having made an impact on the world, but only in the style and manner in which they did so. God has called us *all* to be world-changers, and we will all contribute differently, and in varying degrees, according to the gifts God has given us and the opportunities we are given. To really change the world will cost us our lives as well. Jesus said as much when He said that if we would be His disciples, we must take up our cross and follow Him (Matthew 16:24-25). He has called us to live lives of significance. Indeed, when our course is run it should be said of us that the world is different because we lived in it.

It costs nothing to merely complain about the world's problems. We are called not merely to diagnose but to be a part of the cure, serving as agents of change through the grace and power of God. Our highest duty, our greatest worship, is in living for Him, investing our time, energy, and gifts into the purpose for which we were created (Ephesians 2:10). In reality, it is still just the One man, Jesus Christ, who is changing the world, but He has called each of us to be a part of what He's doing in the earth. We are His body, and it is through us that the life and love of God are revealed to a world still lost outside the Garden. Our mission is simple: whether locally or globally, whether through words spoken or service rendered, whether to many or to few, as occasion allows and God gives grace, go and change the world.

STAINS

For if the blood of bulls and goats and the ashes of a heifer, sprinkling the unclean, sanctifies for the purifying of the flesh, how much more shall the blood of Christ, who through the eternal Spirit offered Himself without spot to God, cleanse your conscience from dead works to serve the living God? (Hebrews 9:13-14)

We used to sing, "What can wash away my Sin?" and the then answer would come, "Nothing but the blood of Jesus." It is a strange concept to those outside the Church, no doubt, that the blood of another person, indeed, the blood of the Son of God, was necessarily spilled to cleanse us from our sin. And yet, the Bible is clear about this. "And according to the law almost all things are purified with blood, and without shedding of blood *there is no remission* (of sins)" (Hebrews 9:22 *emphasis mine*).

It's hard for me to admit it now, but I remember paying $1,700 for a vacuum cleaner. It was a Kirby. I don't even remember inviting the salesman inside the house, but before I knew what was happening, he had squeezed past our defenses and we were signing on the dotted line. It was the presentation that did me in. He passed my vacuum cleaner over the spot on my carpet that he had soiled for the demonstration. After giving mine a good try, all the while extolling the virtues of the Kirby vacuum cleaner, he then proceeded to pass his machine over the same spot. Though I had thought my vacuum cleaner to be pretty good, the evidence was right there in the Kirby! It had gone deeper than my own vacuum cleaner and lifted debris I didn't even know was in my carpet!

Maybe you have seen some of the miracle cleaners sold on those daytime TV infomercials. Whether they are taking tarnish off your silverware, cleaning dirt and grime off an old car, or taking pet stains out of your furniture, each new product holds the promise of a secret that the developers of said product have alone in all the world discovered. Some of these products are probably very good (I believe I do remember hearing some excited housewives giving their testimonials), while others are probably little more than soap and colored water. But one thing they all claim to be able to do is get out those *stubborn* stains. You know, that one you tried with all your might to clean but were unable?

Religion is very much like those cleaners hawked by the daytime infomercial gurus. It promises to give you peace and remove the specter of guilt from your heart. Usually, like those cleaners that promise so much, this amounts to paying some kind of price. If you do the right things, observe certain ceremonies or rituals, and make certain sacrifices, some kind of absolution can be found for your sins and the promised peace you so desire to find can be finally realized. In one sense, religion makes sense. After all, if I have sinned and alienated myself from God, I should have to *do* something to atone for it all. This even has a certain appeal, because if I can clean the slate and pay my debt, I don't owe God anything. We're even.

The problem is that religion and religious duty is kind of like my old vacuum cleaner. It gives the appearance of cleaning things up, superficially at least, but in reality, there is still the shadow of guilt on the heart. We know we somehow don't measure up. Our hearts instinctively know that God is holy, and whatever that may mean, we are not. That is our condition before God, and that is why Jesus came. He alone could be the Lamb of God, the innocent sacrifice who could take upon Himself the sins of the world. None of us could qualify, for we were already stained. He took our place, the innocent for the guilty, and bore the punishment that was rightly ours.

Through His death, He balanced the scales of divine justice on our behalf, serving as the "propitiation (or satisfaction) for our sins, and not for ours only, but also for the whole world" (1 John 2:2). Having fully paid our debt, death had no further claim on Him, since He had no sin of His own. Into that grave the power of God came and He was raised up by the glory of the Father, the Captain of our salvation. And when He was raised up, we were, in a very real sense, raised up with Him. Now, when anyone believes this good news, fully yielding their heart and life to Him, that same power rushes into the tomb of our sin-deadened heart and brings forth a new creation, alive to God and free from the power of sin.

There is no man-made cleaner that can touch the stain of guilt. Good counselors know that guilt is the cornerstone of all mental illness. This is because man was not meant to live outside of fellowship with God. Rather, our life was meant to be lived in response to His love. He alone provides forgiveness through the blood of the cross, for only there was our ransom paid in full. By grace and grace alone we are made right with God through faith (see Romans 5:1). No good deed or life of service can pay such a weighty price. Peace with God cannot be earned. It can only be received as a gift.

Such love demands a response. Either we accept what God has provided through the blood of Christ and respond with appropriate humility, or we reject the grace of God for some charlatan's counterfeit that will never remove the deep stain from our heart. Like many stains we've tried to clean, it fades for a moment only to seep up again and soil the soul with its darkness. The blood of Jesus, however, removes once and for all the stain of sin and opens the way to the Father. That is a door no man can open on His own.

It is only through the sprinkling of Christ's blood that our sins are washed away, the veil is parted, and we are reconciled and reunited with the Father. One may profess to not believe in any of this, but in every person's heart is the desire to be clean; to be rid of the ever present shadow of shame. This cleansing is available, and the price has been paid in full. When the stain of sin is removed from the conscience, it frees us to be the people God has called us to be. There's a new you to be discovered and new life yet to be lived, free from all guilt and cleansed of every stain.

ALL THE WRONG PLACES

For My people have committed two evils:
They have forsaken Me, the fountain of living waters,
And hewn themselves cisterns—broken cisterns that can
hold no water. (Jeremiah 2:13)

I n 1980, the song by Jonny Lee entitled "Lookin' for Love" was
as ubiquitous as the Rubik's Cube, The Brat Pack, and big hair.
It played on all the Country radio stations and served as the main
sound track for the movie, *Urban Cowboy*, starring John Travolta
(who traded in his white disco suit for a cowboy hat and a mechan-
ical bull) and Debra Winger. The first line of the chorus famously
said, "Lookin' for love in all the wrong places," and spoke about the
quest of finding a love that truly satisfies the heart.

As cheesy as this might sound, there is actually something pretty
profound in the concept of the song. The fact is that the story of the
human race is about trying to find that something that truly satisfies
the heart, and all too often, as the song quips, we are looking for
that something "in too many faces." Like the misguided lover in the
song, it seems that mankind is destined to kiss a lot of frogs, and all
too often, still miss our real Prince altogether. There seems to be no

end to the list of things in which we'll try to find some sense of satisfaction: success, money, relationships, sex, alcohol, narcotics, fitness, eastern religions, and hobbies – just to name a few.

After winning his first Wimbledon title at seventeen years of age, Boris Becker found himself feeling empty and contemplating suicide. Harry Patterson, known by his pseudonym, Jack Higgins, author of *The Eagle Has Landed*, famously stated that the one thing he wished someone would have told him is that when you get to the top, there is nothing there. Again and again we hear the tales of the rich and famous who found themselves feeling empty and alone, though they enjoyed what the world calls "success." The long list of celebrity suicides is a grim testimony to the reality that money won't buy you love, meaning, or lasting satisfaction.

The Children of Israel, however, started with the real thing. God has given them a land of their own, blessed and sustained them, and even called them to a special covenant relationship with Himself. Despite God's beneficence and loving kindness, however, the nation was chronically unfaithful, committing idolatry with the false gods of the nations surrounding them. This constantly brought them to ruin, and ultimately they found themselves in exile in foreign lands, captives to the nations that conquered them. To say they learned the hard way would be a tremendous understatement, since they seemed to have to regularly relearn their lesson, as their constant infidelities with other gods continually brought them under the yoke of their neighbors from whom God would deliver them whenever they turned from their sin and called upon His mercies.

Rather than being satisfied with the "well of living water" that God represented, they continually endeavored to create false wells or "broken cisterns" that could never give them what they were looking for. If this sounds familiar, it is because it's the story of every restless generation of mankind since the beginning. Regardless of what we are blessed with, it is never enough, and the endless search goes on for that ultimate and elusive something that will bring everlasting fulfilment and cause all of life to cohere. Yet, it may be worth asking ourselves a reasonable question: "If every generation keeps finding frustration after having searched the world over for what will satisfy, might not the answer be that what we're looking for is not of this world?" Even Solomon, whose resources as Israel's richest king were vast, said that true fulfillment could not be found in what this world offers, though he conducted his search thoroughly. His conclusion was, "And indeed all was vanity and grasping for the wind. There was no profit under the sun" (see Ecclesiastes 2:1-11).

One day Jesus, wearied from his journey, sat beside a well while his disciples went into a neighboring village to find food. As providential occasion would have it, a woman came to the well to draw water. What ensued was a beautiful exchange between Jesus and this woman who had literally been "lookin' for love in too many faces." Instead of coming to the well early in the morning as most of the women would have done, she was there at noon, an outcast due, no doubt, to her reputation. The story of her five failed marriages and current live-in boyfriend could be the story of anyone in our time. It might be your story. Though Jesus was the first to ask for a drink, it was soon revealed that she was the one who was truly thirsty.

Jesus answered and said to her, "Whoever drinks of this water will thirst again, but whoever drinks of the water that I shall give him will never thirst. But the water that I shall give him will become in him a fountain of water springing up into everlasting life." The woman said to Him, "Sir, give me this water, that I may not thirst, nor come here to draw." (John 4:13-15)

I don't believe for one minute that she was just saying that she didn't want to have to trot out to that well for water every day. What she was really saying was that she wanted a drink of that living water Jesus offered that she might end her fruitless search for satisfaction in the broken cisterns to which she had kept returning. Not only did she find her thirst quenched at that well, but her discovery led her entire village to find satisfaction at the same fountain of living waters.

Water is a very conspicuous image, for it is the one thing we cannot live without. It is the source of life, causing even the deserts to bloom when the rain falls upon them. Water represents the answer to those most fundamental needs of the human heart, such as belonging, meaning, and worth. They are all found in the Person of Jesus, who is that fountain of living waters. He, and He alone, meets the deepest needs of the human heart. The choice is ours to either continue drinking from our broken wells or to drink deeply of the life He offers us in Himself. Those who have tried have found that one cannot mix these living waters with any other, for they satisfy only when we leave our broken cisterns behind, once and for all, and choose the life only He can supply. These waters are life. These waters are clean. These waters are free, and as Jesus said, these waters are for "whoever."

INCALCULABLE

Oh, the depth of the riches both of the wisdom and knowledge of God! How unsearchable are His judgments and His ways past finding out! (Romans 11:33)

Today I was listening to an astrophysicist talking about the expansion of the universe. He said that as the universe continues to expand, the speed at which it is expanding grows faster. This is because as stars and other heavenly bodies grow apart from one another, the gravity attracting them to each other weakens, somehow releasing the restraints on the expansion rate of the universe. If that sounds complicated to you, don't worry. You're not alone.

The fact of the matter is, when we consider the heavens and the vast distances between the stars and galaxies, we quickly run into numbers that are so incredibly large that we lose perspective and fail to truly appreciate just how enormous they really are. A simple illustration might suffice to begin to help us understand the kinds of numbers we're talking about. The nearest stars to ours are the three stars in the Alpha Centauri system. From a cosmological perspective, they are very close: only about 4.4 light years away. It even sounds kind of close, doesn't it? However, a light year, of course, is the distance one travels at the speed of light for one year. So, a light year is approximately 5.88 trillion miles. Yes, that is *trillion* with a *T*. So, if you decide to visit, take a big suitcase and plenty of snacks, because our nearest neighbor is somewhere in the range of 24 trillion miles away.

The galaxy that is on record as being furthest from us is 13.3 billion light-years away. Since it takes light from these distant galaxies so long to reach us, looking into our giant telescopes is literally like looking back in time to the very beginnings of our universe. No wonder the Psalmist said,

> When I consider Your heavens, the work of Your fingers,
> The moon and the stars, which You have ordained,
> What is man that You are mindful of him,
> And the son of man that You visit him? (Psalm 8:3-4)

These cosmological realities tell us something of the might and knowledge of God. He is omnipotent, or all-powerful, and omniscient, or all-knowing. However, these are not the greatest, or even the most descriptive, attributes of God. They are impressive, to be sure, but they don't really help us to truly know what God is like. For example, if you asked someone about a particular person and they said, "Oh yes, I know him. He can really bench press a lot," or, "Oh yes, I know him. He's really smart," that would tell you something *about* that person, but you wouldn't really know *him*.

We've all heard stories about our favorite actor or athlete. We can see them on television so much and know their stats so well that we think we really know them. But in reality, knowing all these things *about* these people doesn't mean we really know *them*. In fact, people are often disappointed to find out that the image of the person they idolized is a far cry from what the actual person is like.

God is great, but even more to the point, God is *good*. The Bible is not so much a revelation of the might or wisdom of God, as it is a revelation of His love. In fact, the Bible really is a love story. It's a story of love found and lost and found again. It tells of how man enjoyed perfect communion with God in paradise, only to lose it through his own folly. However, though man was sundered from God by so great a chasm, God was not willing to lose him forever. From the very beginning, the Bible is clear that man is the object of God's love.

When God refers to the vastness of the cosmos which He created, He passes it off in the creation account with the simple statement, "He made the stars also" (Genesis 1:16). Yet He goes into detail about the creation of man, whom He made in His image, according to His likeness" (see Genesis 1:26), placing them in a perfect world where they would have dominion over creation and walk with God. Even in our exile after the fall, God cared for us, working His great redemption plan over the centuries until that moment in which it was consummated through the death, burial, and resurrection of Jesus.

No distance in the heavens can compare with the distance He spanned to reach us in our brokenness, for to reach us God Himself entered the very creation He spoke into existence and became one of us. The Eternal stepped into time and space, and the Immortal took upon Himself flesh and blood. The Almighty became a baby, and the Sinless took upon Himself our sin. The God to whom all creation gives glory bore our shame and was rejected by sinful men. The guiltless Son of God died an ignominious death to pay our ransom.

God is great, but more important to me is the fact that "God is love" (1 John 4:8). He loved us so much that we cannot fully comprehend in our finite state the degree of love that motivated a God to pursue us in our brokenness. But He loves us still, fully, and completely. In one of those paradoxical statements in scripture, the apostle Paul prayed for the Ephesians that they would "know the love of Christ which passes knowledge" (Ephesians 3:19). If one can *know* the *unknowable* and comprehend the incomprehensible, it is through understanding something of the depth of his fathomless love, for it is that love which is truly incalculable.

WHEN SIN DEFILES AND FREEDOMS FADE

...looking carefully lest anyone fall short of the grace of God; lest any root of bitterness springing up cause trouble, and by this many become defiled... (Hebrews 12:15)

In ours or any other society that values freedom, the ideas of personal freedom and corporate responsibility are always held in tension. How much freedom can one exercise before that exercise of freedom infringes upon what is best for the society as a whole? We see these debates going on right now in our nation in regard to gun control, where one group feels that the only way to protect the populace from violence is to limit the freedoms of those wanting to own firearms for personal protection, sport, or recreation. That battle will continue to rage, no doubt, regardless of what laws are passed or fail to pass in the short term.

While those of us who value the right of individuals to own a gun are concerned about the overreach of government and the revocation of our Second Amendment rights, the fact that there is a dialogue in the culture about the issue is a good thing. In fact, that is the whole point of democracy, to give a voice to all sides on any given issue and allow the people to govern themselves through the process of representative government. In fact, the Constitution was written in such a way so as to not be overly restrictive, so the States could determine some of the particulars themselves and the people could make decisions based on the guiding principles the founders provided.

Freedom requires responsibility. Self-government means governing *ourselves* first, which presupposes a personal, moral compass by which we choose good and refuse evil. If we cannot hold ourselves and our passions in check and put the good of society above selfish, personal interests, we cannot hope to maintain a civil society. And yet, we are seeing the breakdown of civility in our society right now. Part of this, of course, is because we have lost our grip on objective moral values. Right and wrong have been redefined to mean whatever we want it to mean, to allow us to indulge in any lifestyle we choose, regardless of its moral or ethical ramifications. The right of the individual, in some cases, has completely usurped the common good. I have to admit, if someone had told me just ten years ago that the nation would be split over whether a man should be allowed to use a woman's public restroom, I wouldn't have believed it. It would have seemed beyond all reason, denying what is universally understood as decent and natural. And yet, that is where we have come as a society.

As the writer of Hebrews tells us, there is a contagious influence to sin. It does not just defile the individual, it can, and often does, defile many. We see this to be true even before the world began. When Satan chose to rebel against God, he did not bear the consequence alone. The Bible tells us that a third of the angels joined him in this rebellion and were cast out of heaven with him as a result (see

Revelation 12:3-9). We worry about the company our children keep because we know, as the scriptures teach, that "bad company corrupts good habits" (1 Corinthians 15:33). We can teach them good values, but the influence of just one friend can undermine all our hard work, causing them to reject the good and the true. The same is true with any society.

Many today wrongly put their trust in what is often called "the better angels of our nature," presupposing man to be inherently good and believing that all he needs is the chance to prove himself and he will see the light and do the right thing, despite all evidence to the contrary. We forget that things once got so bad that God Himself regretted He had ever made man, and rebooted the whole project with Noah and his family after bringing a judgment that wiped out every other living person. When someone called Jesus "good teacher," He challenged him saying, "Why do you call Me good? No one is good but One, that is, God" (Matthew 19:17). In other words, only God is good, and if we take God out of our society, our nation, or our own hearts, we cease to be good in any real sense of the Word. Man, the Bible teaches, is a fallen being, and left to himself, he will seek to gratify his own interests at the expense of others at any cost. We can put up firewalls to contain man's propensity to victimize his fellow man, but all it takes is the first person to breach that wall and a flood of others will follow, whether it's pushing the boundaries of sexual propriety or finding loopholes to exploit weaknesses in the financial markets for one's own profit.

It was Alexis de Tocqueville, who said after visiting the fledgling republic of America, that "Liberty cannot be established without morality, nor morality without faith." We cannot be good without

God, for we are sinful men in a broken world. We will either choose to allow the wicked propensities of men to continue to influence the direction of our culture, running like a mad mob over the precipice of moral dissolution, or we will fall on our faces and cry out for mercies from the God of Heaven. Our Founders chose the latter and built a government based on freedom and personal responsibility, which requires a moral center found only in a biblically grounded faith. Tocqueville also said, "The greatness of America lies not in being more enlightened than any other nation, but rather in her ability to repair her faults." The freedoms we have can allow us to destroy ourselves, or by them we can repair the moral damage we have done to our republic, but we cannot do this trusting in our own goodness.

It was after Benjamin Franklin called the delegates to prayer during the difficult and contentious days of the Constitutional Convention, that the document by which our nation has been governed for 240 years was conceived. It will take that same humility before God to keep us a free people, for freedom requires the acknowledgment of a transcendent law that comes from God. For that law to truly govern us, it must not be merely written in our laws, but inscribed on our hearts through the transforming work of Christ. You don't have to be a Christian to be an American. That's the privilege of a free society. But the grace that enables the members of that society to value the interests of others above their own, and to fight for their freedoms, only comes from God.

LIFE WITHOUT LIMITS

(A Final Word)

A re you interested in living the best life you can live? Of course
you are. We all are. The problem isn't the *want to* so much as
the *how to*. No rational person wants to pass on Jesus' offer to "have
life, and that more abundantly" (John 10:10). So, how do we do it?
How do we take the limits off of life and live it to the full?

Really, the only way to live life without limits is to live a God-de-
signed life. Anything we plan for ourselves, no matter how grand the
plan, is still a man-made life. A life with limits. But a life designed
by God is one in which there is no limitation as to what can be experienced and what can be accomplished. It really comes down to a
simple question of faith, "Who has the better plan for your life, you
or God?"

When God directed Moses to build the tabernacle in the wilderness, He repeatedly told him to build it "according to all that
I show you, that is the pattern of the tabernacle...just so you shall
make it." (Exodus 25:9). God had a plan for the tabernacle, a divine
blueprint that Moses was to follow, and Moses was faithful to follow

God's divine design to the letter. As a result, when Moses finished the work, the glory of God came and filled the tabernacle. God endorsed what Moses did, and He came and dwelt among His people, because Moses had followed God's divine specifications.

I want a life endorsed by God's presence. Just as the children of Israel enjoyed God's presence, power, protection, and provision, because Moses followed God's blueprint for the tabernacle, we too can have a God-blessed life if we will follow God's blueprint for our lives. I want that for myself, and I want that for you too. A life lived according to God's divine design is a life with true purpose, value, and meaning; a life without limits. God not only desires that we live such a life, He made the ultimate investment to ensure that we could experience it, free from all the restrictions with which many of us are all too familiar.

Jesus came to earth, lived His life in absolute obedience to God, and then died in our stead, paying sin's awful price to balance the scales of divine justice, that we might be reconciled to God. Accepting Jesus' sacrifice on your behalf and making Him your personal Lord and Savior is your *connection point* with God's purpose for your life. It all starts there. Regardless of what you have done, you can begin a new life right now (see 2 Corinthians 5:17-18). Your background need not determine your foreground. You can start living His best life for you today. If you are ready to step into a life without limits - a life built according to God's divine specifications, then pray this prayer with all sincerity from your heart...

"Dear Jesus, I believe you came and died in my place, to pay the penalty for my sin. I ask you to come into my heart and make me brand new. I give you my life and declare that you are my Lord, and

I will follow you wherever you lead me. Thank you for dying for me. Father, I accept the gracious gift of forgiveness and receive the new life you have provided for me through Jesus Christ. Thank you for making me your child. A-men."

If you prayed that prayer, I have a few things I want you to do. First of all, tell someone. Let us know. We want to rejoice with you and with the angels in heaven. The Bible says they rejoice over just one sinner who repents. It will make this commitment you've made even more real to you when you share it with others. You can email us at info@wkcconncect.org. Secondly, find yourself a good church and fellowship with others who love Jesus. And lastly, continue to feed yourself daily on God's Word, and spend time fellowshipping with your Heavenly Father. This new life has just begun, and there is SO much to discover. Welcome to a life without limits!

ABOUT THE AUTHOR

Randy Bunch is a pastor, professor, church planter, and author. In his more than thirty years of public ministry, he has pioneered churches on both east and west coasts, traveled extensively throughout the United States, as well as abroad, preaching and teaching God's Word in the power and demonstration of the Holy Spirit.

He has authored several books, including *Healing: The Gospel Truth* and *The Gospel's Saving Power.* Many have also testified to healings from a myriad of maladies, including incurable diseases through Pastor Randy's obedience to a call to the healing ministry.

Currently, in addition to his pastoral duties at West Kern Christian Center, Randy writes extensively and serves as both a staff member and adjunct professor at Summit Bible College in Bakersfield, California. He is a graduate of Rhema Bible Training Center in Broken Arrow, Oklahoma and holds a Masters in Theology from Life Christian University in Tampa, Florida and a Doctorate in Ministry from Summit Bible College in Bakersfield, CA.

Randy's wife, Maria, is a wife, mother, and First Grade teacher with over thirty years' experience, and they are both proud parents and grandparents. They live and serve the Lord in their hometown of Taft, California.

The website of West Kern Christian Center, wkcconnect.org, has an abundance of free resources available, including podcasts, blog posts, an audio healing school, and much more. To contact Pastor Randy to invite him to speak at your church or event, or to find out more about the ministries of West Kern Christian Center, simply contact the ministry at info@wkcconnect.org.

ENDNOTES

1. Harvard T.H. Chan, School of Public Health, "Who Mentored Antwone Fisher," https://sites.sph.harvard.edu/wmy/celebrities/antwone-fisher/ (7 July 2014).

2. Simple to Remember, "Did Life Form By Accident," http://www.simpletoremember.com/articles/a/did-life-form-by-accident/#4 (13 November 2014).

3. Francis Crick, *Life Itself* (New York: Simon and Schuster, 1981), 88.

4. Simple to Remember, "Did Life Form By Accident," http://www.simpletoremember.com/articles/a/did-life-form-by-accident/#4 (13 November 2014).

5. Os Guinness, *The Call* (Nashville: W Publishing Group, 2003), 84. iBooks Edition.

6. Augestine, *Confessions,* (fig-books.com, 2012), 23. iBooks Edition

7. Fred Hoyle, "The Universe: Past and Present Reflections," *Engineering and Science* 45 (November 1981): 8–12.

www.ingramcontent.com/pod-product-compliance
Lightning Source LLC
Chambersburg PA
CBHW071410090426

42737CB00011B/1417